P9-CBD-333

SCIENCE FAIR PROJECTS AND RESEARCH ACTIVITIES

A Comprehensive Guide for Students and Teachers

by Leland Graham
& Isabelle McCoy

Incentive Publications, Inc.
Nashville, Tennessee

Acknowledgements

The authors would like to gratefully acknowledge the assistance and suggestions of the following people: Ianko Chterev, Valerie Crow, Dipan Desai, Drew Kerchenfaut, Jonathan McCoy, Thomas McCoy, Beverly Moody, Sharon Mott, Dan Payne, Virginia Powell, Manuel Rodriguez, John Spilane, Florence Thomas, and John Turner.

Illustrated by Marta Drayton
Cover by Marta Drayton
Edited by Jean K. Signor

ISBN 0-86530-563-3

PRINTED IN THE UNITED STATES OF AMERICA
www.incentivepublications.com

Table of Contents

INTRODUCTION

Science Fair Projects and Research Activities is organized to provide ideas for students, parents, and teachers who are looking for science fair project topics. These science projects and research activities, which normally take twelve to fourteen weeks to complete, are a wonderful way to provide students with some of their most valuable learning experiences based on biochemistry, botany, chemistry, computer science, earth and space sciences, environmental sciences, medicine and health, microbiology, physics, and zoology.

Some of the featured activities, such as taking notes, making an outline, creating a bibliography, and preparing an abstract have been designed so that they can be used as individual *or* group activities; however, other activities require individual participation. Carefully read the instructions before beginning each chapter.

Since research is an integral part of a science project, students will be carefully guided through a step-by-step process of developing the abstract, introductory paragraph, body, and conclusion of their research paper. Included in this book is an example of a research paper for teachers to use as a guide for students.

A backboard section, also included in this book, is especially important for the actual science fair. Even though a student's knowledge and understanding in writing the research paper may be excellent, if the backboard materials are not correctly displayed, the science fair project will not receive the proper recognition. To further assist students, the authors have included examples of various types of lettering, design elements, and sample backboard sketches.

The Appendix contains a collection of forms: tips for parents, sample letters to parents and students, a research proposal sheet, judges' score sheet, science project resources, and a reproducible certificate. Finally, we have included some reproducible title cards which can be printed on card stock for use on the backboard.

Chapter One

SCIENCE FAIR CATEGORIES

Science Fair Categories

When beginning work on a science fair project, it is important to focus on the various categories. On this and on the following pages, there are descriptions of each category. Following each category are pictures, charts, graphs, or headlines representing the category that might inspire a topic choice. Chapter Fifteen has backboard project examples for each category.

1. Biochemistry

Biochemistry is the branch of biology that involves the chemistry of life processes, such as molecular biology, molecular genetics, blood chemistry, photosynthesis, protein chemistry, and food chemistry. In recent years, due to the evolvement of powerful scientific instruments, biochemistry now includes ways to synthesize molecules that duplicate those of living systems as well as molecules that are able to perform entirely new functions.

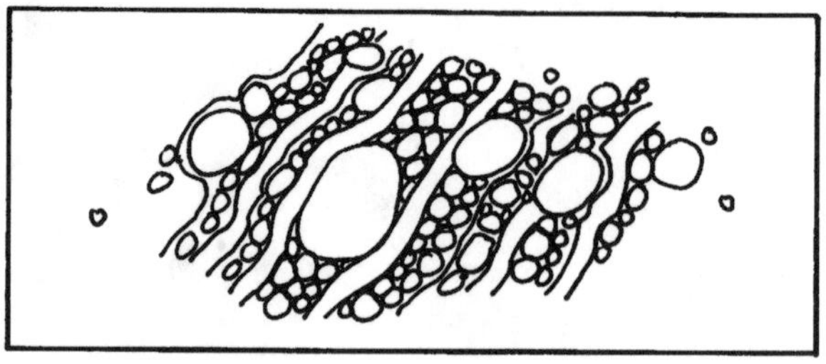

Therefore, biochemistry, while increasingly significant in our modern society as a distinct field of research, is also combining with other biological disciplines. The development of such new areas of study as cell biology and molecular biology reflects this integration. Increasingly, present problems in the biological sciences are being resolved by team efforts of skilled scientists from many disciplines who have mastered their once-separate fields.

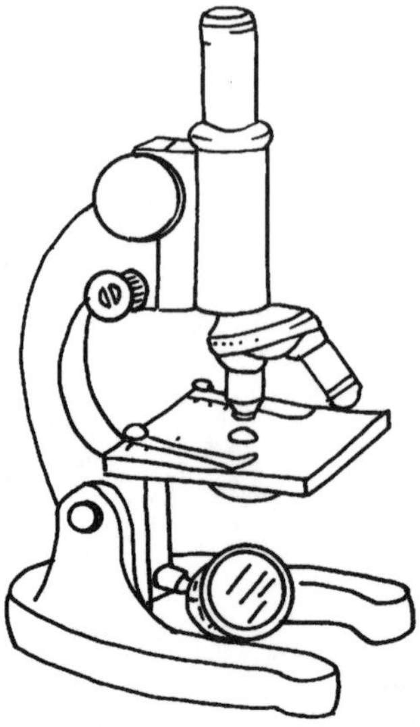

2. Botany

Even in prehistoric societies, people were interested in plants as sources of useful products. The first records of scientific botany are from the ancient Greeks and Romans.

Botany, the study of plant life, may be approached from many directions, each of which is a specialization involving an aspect of plant life. Examples of these specializations include classification, form and structure, life processes and functions, diseases, fossils, and heredity and variation. Botany includes the study of agriculture, agronomy, forestry, horticulture, plant taxonomy, plant physiology, plant pathology, plant genetics, and hydroponics.

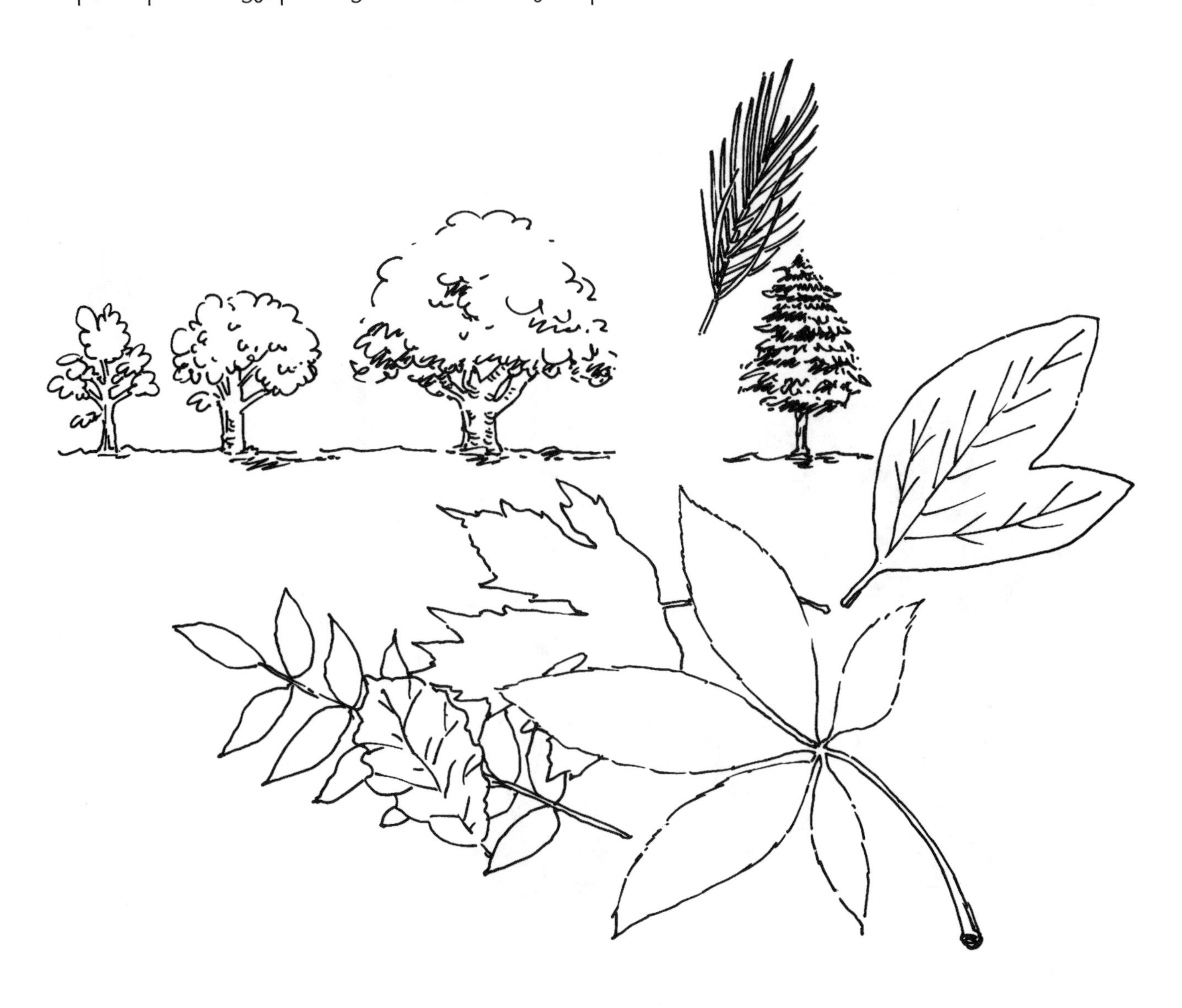

3. Chemistry

Chemistry is the physical science that deals with the composition, structure, and properties of materials and also the changes that these substances endure. Because the study of chemistry includes the entire universe, it is the key to the understanding of the other sciences. You may want to consider for your science fair project these branches of chemistry: physical chemistry, organic chemistry, inorganic chemistry, and soil chemistry. Other choices might include topics related to materials, plastics, fuels, pesticides, and metallurgy.

The four basic needs of people—shelter, clothing, food, and medical services—are closely linked with chemistry. The future of chemistry lies in providing solutions to such problems as the creation of new energy sources and the elimination of disease, famine, and pollution; therefore, chemistry provides the key to improving the environment and raising world living standards.

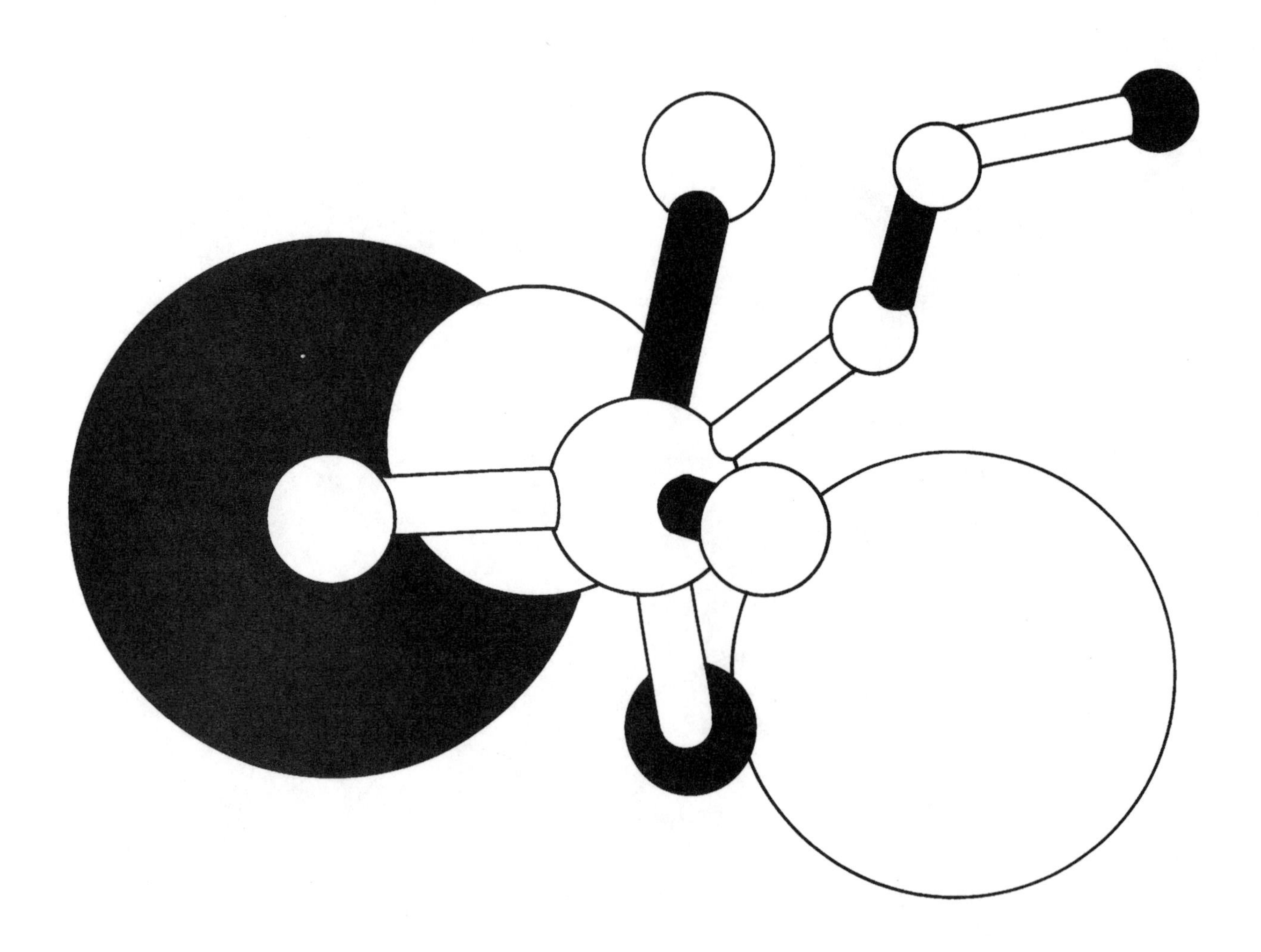

4. Computer Science

Computer science is associated with the study and use of computers and computer-based processes. The three types of computers are digital, analog, and hybrid. Digital computers function internally and perform operations exclusively with digital numbers. Analog computers use variable parts to accomplish their built-in operations. Hybrid computers are less common and use both variable and digital techniques in their operation.

Computer science involves the study and development of computer software and hardware. This category of computer science includes computer design and programming and intersects with a number of other disciplines such as mathematics, information theory, and electronic engineering.

5. Earth and Space Science

In its strictest form, the term *Earth Science* is synonymous with geology, the study of the lithosphere (solid part) of the Earth. Commonly, however, Earth Science also includes the study of the Earth's other divisions, the atmosphere and hydrosphere, as well as the planet's environment in space. Thus, it refers to broad, interrelated studies that encompass astronomy and astrophysics, mineralogy, oceanography, meteorology, climatology, and seismology.

The ultimate goal of Earth Science is to solve the mystery of the origin and evolution of our planet. In working toward this end, scientific disciplines and fields of study that encompass the space beyond the earth's atmosphere are employed. Earth Science, therefore, turns up as an influence on our lives in many unexpected ways.

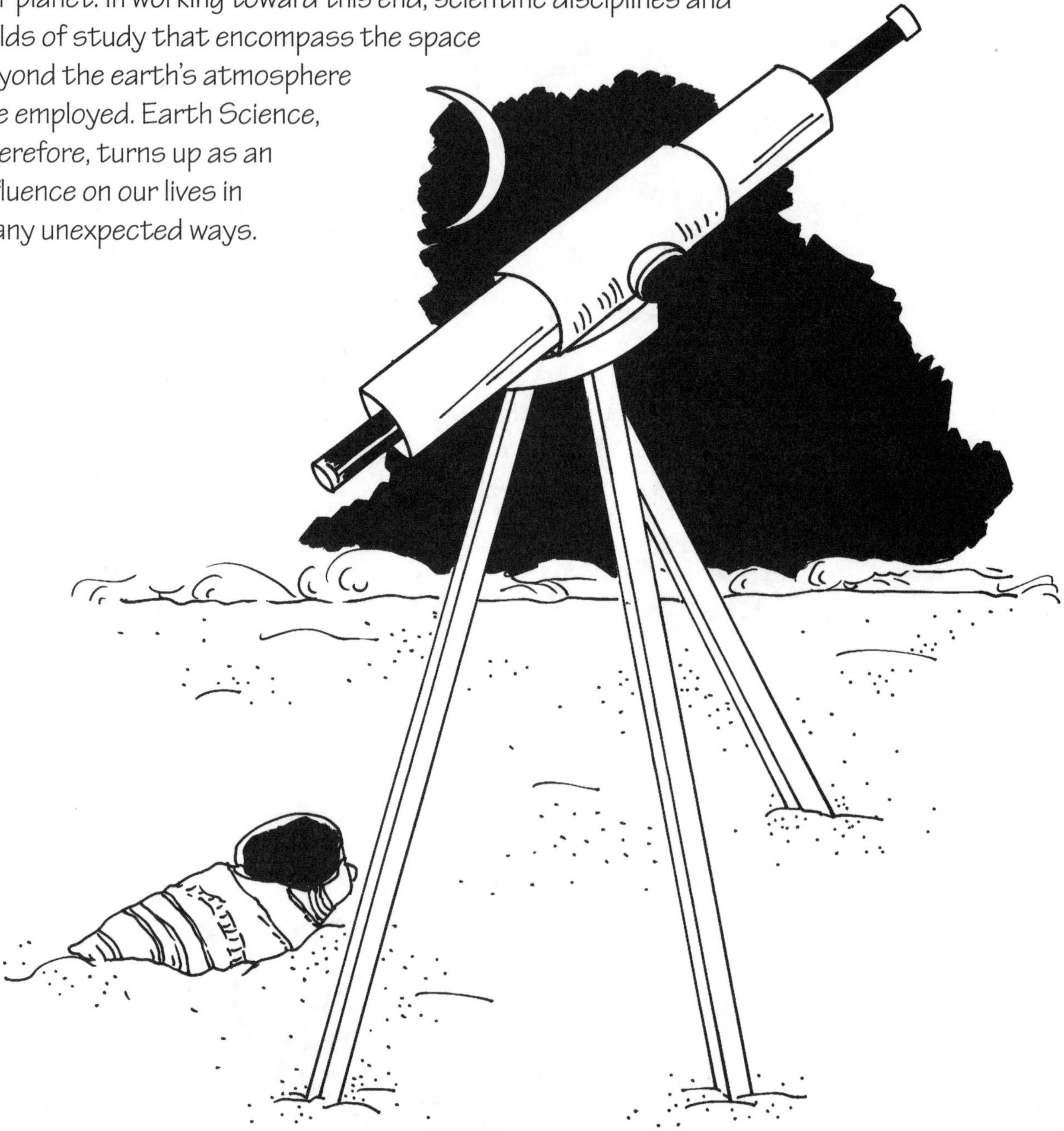

6. Environmental Science

Environmental Science is the study of the interaction of living things with their chemical, physical, and biological environment. Ecosystems in their entirety are complex, and, therefore, ecological studies of parts of ecosystems or individual ecosystems are made. From those studies, connections between different systems can be established. In this way, ecologists try to explain the ways larger ecosystems work.

Important ecological concepts have influenced conservation. Some ecologists question the role of humans in the environment: Are people dependent on, or independent of nature? Environmental Science is seen as both a social and a scientific subject providing a connection between human and physical environments.

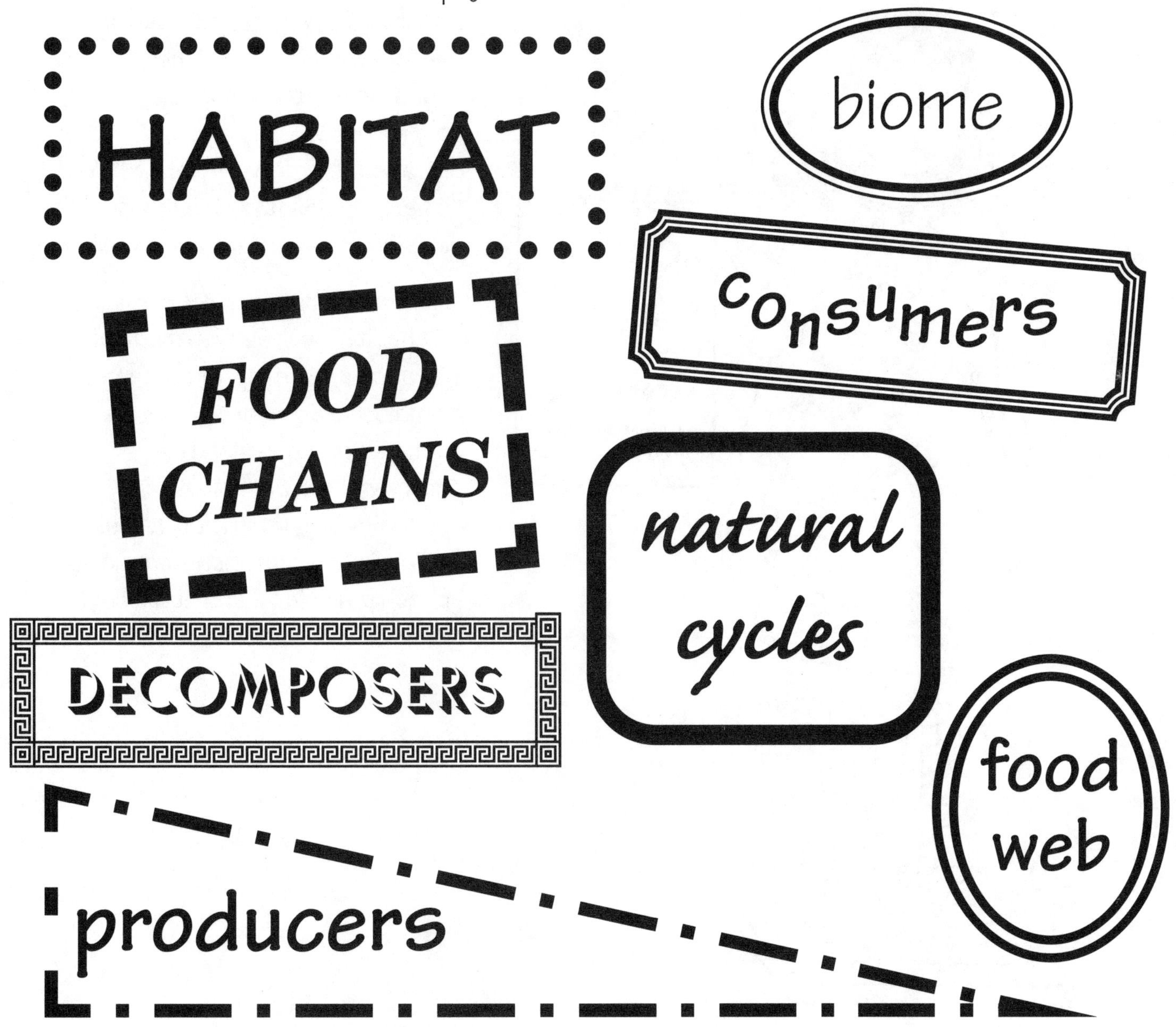

7. Medicine and Health

The practice of medicine is dedicated to the continuation of good health. This involves detecting and preventing disease, curing those disorders for which treatment exists, and lessening pain and minimizing disabilities. Modern medicine has also assumed the role of improving public health by promoting hygiene and advancing standards for nutrition and the environment. Public health is the effort coordinated by society to safeguard the health of its members.

On all levels, the major concerns of public health agencies are the guarantee of disease-free food and water and adequate sanitation systems. In addition, other concerns are the prevention or control of epidemic and endemic diseases, the delivery of health care to needy population groups, and the devising of laws regarding health.

Thus, the category of medicine and health involves the study of diseases and health of humans and animals. Its branches include some of the following: dentistry, pharmacology, pathology, ophthalmology, nutrition, radiology, pediatrics, dermatology, cardiology, speech pathology, and audiology.

8. Microbiology

Microbiology is the study of microscopic organisms. It is the biology of microorganisms, such as bacteriology, virology, protozoology, fungi, bacterial genetics, and yeast. The field of microbiology was greatly advanced in the 1930s with the development of the electron microscope, which allowed the observation of viruses. Most genetic research on the biochemical level since the mid-20th century has used viruses as the experimental organism of choice. Modern microbiology has contributed greatly to the study of disease and to research in agriculture and environmental health.

Bacteria Found in Shellfish Can Cause Death

BEWARE: Toxic Mold

NEW STUDY: Antibiotics Not A Cure For Chronic Lyme Disease

Too Much Rain Causing Plant Fungus

Back Bugging You? May Be Microorganisms

9. Physics

Physics is the basis of all other physical sciences and much of technology. Physicists' view of the world has changed drastically due to two major developments: Einstein's theory of relativity and the quantum and atomic theories. Almost every field of physics is divided into experimental and theoretical areas. Now, in the 21st century, a physicist rarely uses both of these approaches because the techniques have become extremely specialized.

In each field of physics where research is under way, there exists a body of knowledge, laws, and principles that have been verified experimentally. Physics involves theory, principles, and laws governing energy and the effect of energy on matter. It will include such topic areas as solid states, optics, acoustics, particles, nuclear energy, atomic energy, plasma, superconductivity, fluid and gas dynamics, thermodynamics, semiconductors, magnetism, electricity, and biophysics.

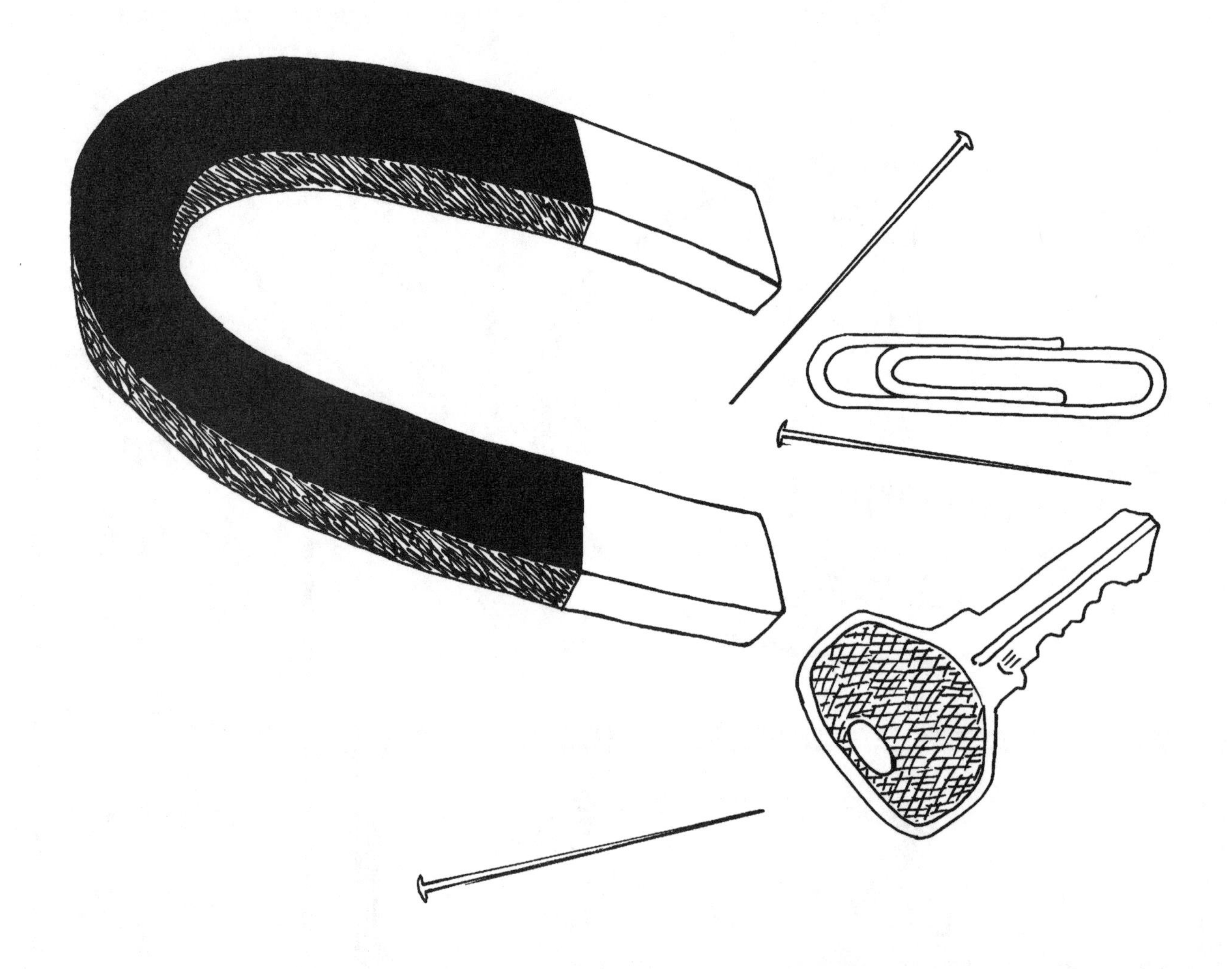

10. Zoology

Certain aspects of zoology, the study of animals, are more encompassing than others because they embrace all four cornerstones: taxonomy, anatomy, physiology, and genetics. Taxonomy is the science of classification; anatomy deals with the structure of organisms; physiology encompasses the function of organisms; and genetics deals with heredity. Although zoology is a science in its own right, it is increasingly becoming secondary as a discipline of study to the concept of general biology.

Zoology includes ornithology, ichthyology, herpetology, entomology, paleontology, cellular physiology, cytology, histology, and animal physiology, genetics, husbandry, and ecology. It also includes the study of invertebrates.

Disease-Carrying Asian Tiger Mosquitoes Found in Southern California

State of Emergency Declared in Siberia: Locust Invasion

What Became Of The Dinosaurs?

Central African Chimps Threatened with Extinction

Chapter Two

SELECTING A TOPIC

Selecting the Topic

The most important step in creating a science project is choosing an appropriate topic. In selecting a topic, refer to the ten science categories described in Chapter One. Use the guidelines below in choosing a topic.

1. Avoid a topic that is too broad.

   EXAMPLE: **What Things Affect Ice?**

   A topic which is too broad makes it impossible to find all the information that is needed to adequately cover the topic.

   BETTER TOPIC: **What are the Effects of Salt and Sawdust on the Brittleness of Ice?**

2. Avoid a topic that is too limited.

   EXAMPLE: **What is Solar Energy?**

   A student cannot write a report on a topic that can be explained in a few words or a sentence.

   BETTER TOPIC: **What is the Feasibility of Using Solar Energy?**

3. Avoid a topic that is dangerous or illegal.

   A topic that is dangerous or illegal probably will not be given permission to be admitted.

4. Avoid a topic on which people throughout the world cannot agree.

   EXAMPLE: **What is the Best Music?**

   A topic should be supported with facts.

   BETTER TOPIC: **How Does Classical Music Affect Student Performance?**

5. Avoid a topic which is confusing because it is not clear what information is requested.

   EXAMPLE: **Why Do We Have Earthworms?**

   A topic should not be a simple report; instead, you should be able to perform a test or experiment using the scientific method.

   BETTER TOPIC: **How do Worms Affect Plant Growth?**

What Makes a Good Science Project?

A good science project topic is one which enables you to conduct experiments related to it. A science fair project is more than just researching a topic, writing a report, building a model, and making a graph. Once a topic is chosen, decide if it is a good one by using the following guidelines:

1. **Decide if you are really interested in the topic.**
   A good science fair project is an experiment—that means it is a test to detect a solution to a question that you have. Use your experiences.
   Do you remember a time when you noticed something and thought, "I wonder how that works?" or "I wonder what would happen if . . .?"
   Why not turn that question into a science fair project? For example, if you are interested in insects and you see some ants moving quickly on a warm day, you might ask yourself, "What effect does temperature have on the rate at which insects move?"

2. **Conduct a test to find an answer to a question.**
   Use the scientific method—do not use simple reports or demonstrations. They show only your knowledge on a topic.
   For example, if you want to know which grows faster, hair or fur, you can conduct an experiment to find the answer. A good question can be answered only by measuring something. In this example, measuring the rate of growth for both hair and fur is a way to determine the answer for your question.

3. **Complete your project without the assistance of parents and teachers.**
   Do a project because it is fun and rewarding. Someone else's help detracts from the enjoyment and lessons to learn.

4. **Think of new things you want to know.**
   Look at newspapers or magazines. Think about current events, such as hunger in Africa during a drought *("What Kind of Plants Grow During a Drought?")*, the ozone hole over Antarctica *("How Can We Reduce Ozone?")*, or an oil spill in the Pacific Ocean *("How Can Oil Be Removed from Our Oceans?")*. You can use one of those topics to research.
   One way to recognize a good project is to see if the results make you think of other questions. If so, that is a great project!

Name ________________________________

Recognizing Poor Science Topics

The topics below are poor choices for a science fair project. On the line beneath each topic, write the reason why it should not be chosen.

1. What elements comprise water?

   ____

2. What would be the best way to improve things?

   ____

3. What is an erupting volcano?

   ____

4. Ants in our environment.

   ____

Creating a Good Topic

Directions: In order to create a good topic, complete each question by filling in the blanks.

Examples: How do various types of water affect the growth of plants?
What effect does salt have on the boiling point of various liquids?
Which type of seed do birds prefer?

5, How do /does ________________ affect ________________________?

6. What effect do /does ________________ have on ____________________?

7. Which type of ____________ do __________ prefer?

8. What ____________________ are preferred by __________________?

9. Which ______________ lasts longest?

10. Which ______________ is more effective for ______________________?

Choosing a Topic

(To the Teacher)

Objectives:

1. The students will select a topic and write an appropriate statement or question for their science fair project.
2. The students will conduct a preliminary science fair search to determine the availability of materials for the project.

Procedures:

1. In class, have a brainstorming session to list topics of current interest.
   a. Eliminate irrelevant science fair topics.
   b. Eliminate topics that are too broad or too limited
   c. Eliminate topics that are not original.
   d. Rewrite topics as necessary.
2. Have students continue brainstorming at home in order to select a topic that interests them.
3. Have students complete Section I of the Research Proposal Sheet (Appendix, p. 113).
4. Ask students to go to the library and search for information to answer the proposed question or statement. Have students list the available sources on the back of the proposal sheet. Do not forget to suggest the Reader's Guide, periodicals, almanacs, encyclopedias, letters, and books on the subject. List ideas for conducting surveys, interviews, observations, and experiments. Decide on other appropriate science fair methods for gathering information such as visiting areas of significance, taking photos, or writing letters.
5. Ask students to complete Section II of the Research Proposal Sheet (see page 113).
6. After approval, students complete Section III of the Research Proposal Sheet (see page 113) to outline strategies.
7. Ask students to have a parent or guardian sign the proposal sheet.

Evaluation:

The students will successfully write a research statement or question and an outline of strategies that meets the teacher's approval.

Chapter Three

SUGGESTED SCIENCE FAIR TOPICS

Suggested Science Fair Topics

The following are suggested topics for science fair projects. Students may select from this list, or they may create their own topic.

Biochemistry

What is the relationship between the amount of pectin in fruits and the amount of juice they contain?
Can the colors of natural dyes be separated using chromatin paper?
How is the jelling of gelatin affected by the type of fruit used?
What are the effects of a low-fat diet on cholesterol?
How does ultraviolet light affect green bean seed germination?
What are the effects of stored temperature on the amount of Vitamin C retained in oranges?
What are the effects of dye and bleach on hair?
What are the toxic effects of plastic packaging on earthworms?
What is the relationship between carbon dioxide production and temperature in yeast growth?
What are the optimum storage conditions for viable corn seed development?

Botany

What is the percentage of water in various fruits and vegetables?
Does music affect plant growth?
What are the effects of sound on plants?
Compare types of artificial light on plant growth?
What are the best conditions for mushroom production/growth of ferns?
What are the transpiration rates for different plants and conditions?
What are sugar levels in plant sap at different times and dates?
What factors affect seed germinatio?
What factors affect flowering?
What factors affect nodule formation in legumes?
Can household compounds be used to promote good health in plants?
What are the effects of cigarette smoke on plants?
What are the effects of phosphates on aquatic plants?
What are the effects of solar activity on plants?
How do different conditions affect the speed at which vegetables and fruit ripen?
How do different types of fertilizers affect plant growth?
How do different treatments change how fast seeds sprout?
How close does a pesticide have to be to protect a plant?
What effect does seed size have on plant growth?
Which type of food molds the fastest?
How do different types of plant food affect plant growth?
What factors affect plant reproduction?
What are the effects of soil components and organic matter on the growth of plants?

Chemistry

Study chemical change and the factors that affect the rate such as heat, light, or catalysts.
Acid and basic solutions—How can they be modified? What are the practical considerations in lakes, food, or soil?
What are some factors affecting glassmaking?
What are the effects of cola on teeth?
Which type of soda is the most corrosive?
Which is worse for your teeth—cola, orange juice, or vinegar?
What are the effects of different substances on crystals?
Which toothpaste works best?
Does the processing of food produce gas?
If bacteria are not present, will the rate of rusting on iron decrease?
What are the effects of temperature on viscosity of oil?
Which is the most effective consumer product—glues, stain removers, antiseptics, mouthwashes, detergents, paper towels, or plastic wraps?
Compare the pH levels in the mouths of various animals and humans at different times of day.
Analyze snow and rain from different areas for pollutants.
What are the effects of salt and other contaminants on the rates of rusting?
What are the factors that affect the rate and size of crystal growth?
Analyze soil samples for their components, ability to hold moisture, or pH.
Does the amount of particle pollution vary with distance from a road, location, or with height?
What are the effects of salts on the freezing points of liquids?
What factors affect the firing of clay?
What are the effects of electric fields on the rate of evaporation of liquids?
What affects the rising of bubbles in a liquid?

Computer Science

Study computer storage and retrieval techniques.
What ways can computers may be used in the classroom?
What are some procedures and techniques for manipulating data and information?
Create a computer simulation.
Create a programmable processing unit design, function, or operation.
Develop a video game.
Develop a new program to write a new custom program.
Study the use of computers in managing an industrial process.

Earth and Space Science

Where is the current of a stream faster?
Do the moon's phases affect Earth's weather?
Snow—What happens when it melts? What does it contain? What is the structure of a snowflake?
How much dew is formed on a square meter over a period of time? What causes the variations in the amounts?
What is the make-up of frost and dew?
What affects the rate of evaporation the most—temperature, humidity, wind speed, or other factors?
Does fresh water hold heat longer than salt water?

Earth and Space Science *continued*

What factors affect the cooling of land?
Is there a relationship between sunspot cycles and earthquakes?
Compare the load bearing strength of different soils.
What are the effects of weather on human emotions?
What are the factors affecting ice patterns on glass?
Compare size and air resistance of model cars in a wind tunnel.
Which angle of launch sends a projectile the greatest distance?
Design a better parachute.
How does soil pH affect the pH of water that touches soil?
Does soil type change how well plants grow?
How are different soil types affected by water running over them?

Environmental Science

How does acid rain affect lakes?
What type of soil is best for water retention?
What are the effects of carbon monoxide on a roadside?
What are the effects of various bacteria in different types of soil?
What is the impact of pollution on an ecosystem?
Find efficient methods of breaking down crude oil in seawater.
Find effective methods of harvesting and using plankton.
What are the effects of air pollution on algae, protozoa, fish, insects, or mosses and lichens?
What are the effects of smog on city flora?
Study the relationship between vegetation and insects.
What are some air purification methods?
Experiment with biodegradability
What are the effects of herbicide spraying?
Conduct an ecological study of the animal and plant life occupying the same tree.
What are the effects of crowding (with the same or different species) on a certain plant?
What is the relationship of soil type and vegetation?

Medicine and Health

Is there a relationship between eating breakfast and school performance?
On which foods does fungus grow best?
How do acids affect teeth?
Do different varieties of the same fruit have the same level of Vitamin C?
Do different brands of orange juice have the same amount of Vitamin C?
Are there different amounts of iron in different breakfast cereals?
What effects do different amounts of exercise have on the production of carbon dioxide in humans?
What is the relationship between physical exercise and learning ability?
What factors affect the strength of hair growth?
Will practice increase jumping height?
Will various herbs increase memory?

Microbiology

What is the effectiveness of antiseptics and soaps on household bacteria?
What are the effects of disinfectants on bacteria?
What is the antimicrobiological effect of garlic?
What are the effects of nicotine and caffeine on the growth of bacteria?
What happens to the way plants grow if there are no microorganisms in the soil?
Are different plants affected in different ways by specific microorganisms?
What are some things that produce mutations in bacteria, yeast, protozoa, and molds?
Do mouthwashes kill microbes?
What are the effects of toothpaste on bacteria?
What is the effectiveness of antimicrobial agents on microbes?
Experiment with microbial degradation of petroleum.
What factors affect the growth of bacteria?

Physics

What factors affect burning?
Compare strengths of nylon fishing lines.
Compare the efficiency/effects of various lubricants on gears.
Which homemade airplane design flies best?
What factors affect the bounce of a dropped ball?
What affects light reflection? refraction? diffraction?
What affects the pitch/volume of sound?
What factors affect the voltage/amperage/resistance of electric circuits?
How does temperature change affect the elasticity of rubber/the effectiveness of glue?
How does temperature change affect paint?
What are the effects of solar activity on radio waves/microwaves?
Factors affecting sound dampening
Study the physics of ski waves.
How do metals compare in conducting heat?

Zoology

How does electricity affect fruit flies?
How do different types of liquids affect fruit fly growth?
What are the reactions of protozoa to changes in the environment?
Study the stimuli that attract mosquitoes.
What are the factors affecting the rate at which a cricket chirps?
How does pH affect brine shrimp?
How does acid rain affect goldfish?
How do ants behave around various other insects?
How do earthworms affect our soil?
Which grows faster—hair or fur?
Which type of treats do dogs prefer?
Does alcohol affect a spider's ability to spin its web?
Do vitamins enhance the growth of gerbils?
Do mice really like cheese?

Chapter Four

SUGGESTED SCIENCE PROJECT DEADLINES

Science Project Timetable

12 Weeks Before the Fair **Date** ________________

_____ Choose a topic and have it approved.

_____ Make a list of resources (libraries, interviews, letters, internet sites).

_____ Select reading materials that are appropriate to topic.

11 Weeks Before the Fair **Date** ________________

_____ Organize information and narrow the focus in order to form a hypothesis on a testable idea.

_____ Write, call, and e-mail for additional information and/or help from business firms, government agencies, and universities.

_____ Start a bound log book for keeping records. Write down everything completed , thought, and observed about the topic and experimentation. Date each entry.

_____ Write out a research plan before beginning the project. Include problem, hypothesis, procedure, and bibliography.

_____ Talk to an adult sponsor and obtain the forms and signatures needed.

10 Weeks Before the Fair **Date** ________________

_____ Collect materials and equipment, select an appropriate work site, and carefully follow all safety regulations.

_____ Learn how to use any apparatus required for the project. Seek expert guidance whenever possible.

_____ Set up the investigation/experiment.

_____ Keep log book current.

9 Weeks Before the Fair **Date** ________________

_____ Begin testing, experimenting, or constructing.

_____ Adjust research plan as information is obtained from expert sources. Check with your sponsor first for approval of any changes.

_____ Add information to log book as experiment/project continues.

8 Weeks Before the Fair Date ________________

______ Continue collecting data.

______ Continue recording notes and observations.

______ Take photographs of the research project in progress.

______ Continue research for background information about the topic.

______ Become the expert.

7 Weeks Before the Fair Date ________________

______ Continue experimentation.

______ Begin work on first draft of written report (statement of problem, hypothesis, preliminary information, bibliography).

______ Continue recording notes and making observations.

______ Continue taking photographs of research project.

6 Weeks Before the Fair Date ________________

______ Continue experimentation.

______ Consult experts contacted earlier as needed.

______ Review books and articles for additional ideas.

______ Continue recording notes and making observations.

______ Take photographs of final stages of research project.

______ Discuss work completed on research paper.

5 Weeks Before the Fair Date ________________

______ Begin preparing titles, labels, and photographs for the backboard.

______ Start the analysis of data collected.

______ Begin designing charts, graphs, or other visual aids for the backboard and for the written report.

______ Continue writing first draft of research paper, including the section on your experimental procedure.

Adapted from International Rules for Precollege Science Research: Guidelines for Science and Engineering Science Fairs, 2000–2001.

4 Weeks Before the Fair **Date** ________________

_____ Review analysis of data and results obtained.

_____ Write second draft of research paper to include analysis of information, evaluation of possible solutions, conclusion, and presentation of results.

3 Weeks Before the Fair **Date** ________________

_____ Finish constructing and designing the display board.

_____ Begin writing the text for background information to be used on the display and plan the layout.

_____ Complete charts, graphs, and visual aids.

_____ Work on the draft of written research paper.

_____ Write an abstract for the project using 250 words or less.

2 Weeks Before the Fair **Date** ________________

_____ Write another draft of research paper.

_____ Finalize background text by using concise wording and bullets. Mount text on backboard.

_____ Check and double check the backboard for spelling, punctuation, and grammar.

_____ Mount graphs, charts, drawings, and photographs on the backboard.

_____ Check rules governing display materials and allowable apparatus.

_____ Write or type final research paper.

1 Week Before the Fair **Date** ________________

_____ Proofread the written or typed research paper.

_____ Set up the display at home in order to check for any flaws or mistakes.

_____ Practice presenting the research and answering questions with an expert.

_____ Make sure all forms needed are completed: log book; written or typed research paper; abstract; and backboard.

Adapted from International Rules for Precollege Science Research: Guidelines for Science and Engineering Science Fairs, 2000–2001.

Chapter Five

FORMAT AND STEPS FOR THE RESEARCH PAPER

Format and Steps for the Research Paper

A paper describing project research is required and should be displayed in the research project notebook, along with any necessary forms, or other relevant materials. Before beginning, check for any special rules that the teacher may require. A good research paper includes the following sections:

1. **Title Page**—Project title, student's name, address, school, and grade.
2. **Table of Contents**—When a section is complete, number each section.
3. **Introduction**—The introduction should explain the background information about the topic and the reason behind the choice of study. Refer to previous research as well as the project experiments. Establish a strong rationale for the study by emphasizing unresolved issues or questions. Conclude by stating the research hypothesis.
4. **Materials and Procedure**—Describe in detail the methods used to derive the data and observations. Use photographs and drawings of the equipment to further describe the experiment(s). Include a precise description of the sample, any apparatus that was constructed or modified for the study, and methods of data collection.
5. **Results**—Present the data collected in the experiment, in tables and graphs; summarize the data in narrative form. Include statistical analysis of the data. Do not include raw data. Include only information collected during the current year's study.
6. **Discussion**—The results and conclusions should flow smoothly and logically from the data. Be thorough. Compare results with theoretical values, published data, commonly held beliefs, and/or expected results. A complete paper should include a discussion of possible errors or problems experienced.
7. **Conclusion**—Briefly summarize the results. Discuss whether or not the data supported the hypothesis and what the next steps in experimentation may be.
8. **Acknowledgements/Credits**—Credit assistance received from mentors, parents, teachers, and other sources.
9. **References/Bibliography**—The reference list should include any material from outside sources (i.e., books, websites, papers, journal articles, and communications cited in the paper). Follow the samples shown in the bibliography section.
10. **Appendix**—Include critical information that is too lengthy for the main section of the paper, such as raw data, additional tables and graphs, copies of surveys and tests, and diagrams of specified equipment.

Chapter Six

USING THE SCIENTIFIC METHOD

The Scientific Method

The scientific method is a step-by-step procedure which is used to determine the answer to any scientific question. Below are the six steps in the scientific method.

1. **PROBLEM:** .... Identify a problem or question to investigate.

2. **HYPOTHESIS:** .... State what the result of the investigation might be.

3. **MATERIALS:** .... State the materials used in the experiment.

4. **PROCEDURE:** .... Complete a step-by-step explanation of the experiment. Follow the steps to test the hypothesis.

5. **RESULTS:** .... Make observations and take notes about the observations.

6. **CONCLUSION:** .... Reach a conclusion based on observations and data analysis.

The Importance of The Scientific Method

ıethod will allow a sensible problem-solving approach
ɜstion. If a problem emmerges, or the experiment
the scientific method will provide remedies to make
ı the experiment. Another important factor is that it
ɜt to repeat or copy another scientist's experiment. If
cannot be copied, then the conclusions derived from the
nent are questioned. In this way, the scientific method
eriments and conclusions to be duplicated.

Chapter Seven

BIBLIOGRAPHY CARDS AND NOTE TAKING

Bibliography Cards

If a student plans to use information from a particular source (book, encyclopedia, magazine, Internet, interview, surveys, or pamphlets), he or she must record and keep certain information for the bibliography. The information can be recorded on 3" x 5" index cards, which will make it easier to create a bibliography.

When writing bibliography cards, write a number in the upper right-hand corner of each note card for easy organization and reference. Depending on the type of resource used, different information will need to be recorded on the bibliography card.

Record the following information for a book:

1. Name of the author (last name first)
2. Title of the book (underlined)
3. Place of publication (city)
4. Name of the publisher
5. Year of publication (most recent year)

9

Skelsey, Alice. Growing Up Green. New York: Workman Publishing Company. 1973.

Note: *A comma is placed between the author's last and first names. A period is pl the author's name and book title. A colon is placed after the city, and a comma is ins between the publisher and the year. A period is placed after the year.*

Record the following information for an encyclopedia:

1. Name of the author of the article (if there is an author)
2. Title of the article (in quotation marks)
3. Title of the encyclopedia (underlined)
4. Year of publication (edition)

12

Thompson, Joe. "Herbicides."
The New Book of Knowledge.
1983 ed.

Note: *If the article has an author, a comma is placed between the author's last and first names. A period is placed after the entire name. A period is placed at the end of article title and before the closing quotation marks. A period is also placed after the name of the encyclopedia.*

7

"Lion." World Book Encyclopedia
1996. ed.

Record the following information for a magazine or newspaper:

1. Name of the author (if one is given)
2. Title of the article (in quotation marks)
3. Name of the magazine or newspaper (underlined)
4. Date of the magazine or newspaper
5. Page number(s) of the article

10

Smithfield, Mary. "Solar Activity." Scientific American. 4 September, 2004: 67-70.

Note: *A comma is placed between the author's last and first names. A period is placed after the entire name. A comma is placed between the month and year. The date is followed by a colon. A period is placed after the page number(s). If the article begins on one page but is continued on a non-consecutive page, a comma is inserted between the page numbers (e.g., 84, 97, 99). If the article appears on consecutive pages, a hyphen is inserted between the page numbers (e.g., 84–87).*

14

"West Nile Virus Spreading South." Atlanta Journal. 26 December, 1985.

Note: *The above example illustrates an unsigned newspaper article. The punctuation remains the same.*

Record the following information for a computer reference:

If referencing a magazine article from the computer, follow the format for writing a bibliography card for a magazine article.

If referencing an encyclopedia from the computer, follow the format for writing an encyclopedia bibliography card.

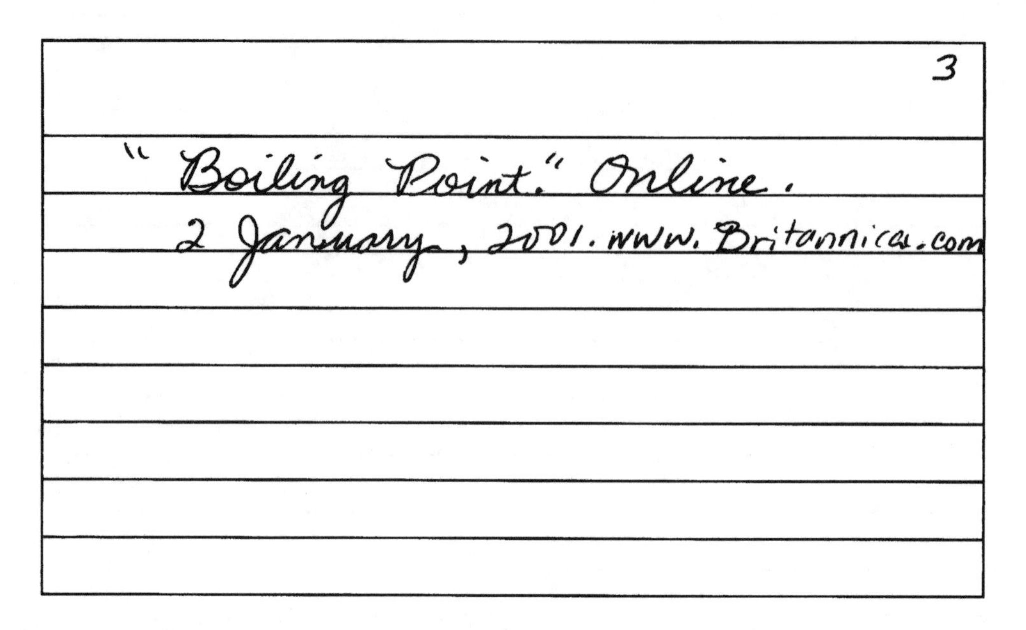

Note: *Bibliography cards need to be made if dictionaries, atlases, almanacs, audiotapes, videotapes, television programs, movies, interviews, letters, surveys, or the Internet are used. Ask a teacher for assistance.*

Note Taking

Note taking is a shortcut for writing down information that has been read and needs to be remembered. Taking notes is a very important process when writing a research paper; one cannot expect to remember all that is read.

Some writers choose to take notes on note sheets such as the sample note sheet on page 42. Others decide to take notes on index cards or slips of paper, using a different card for each main idea. Here are some helpful hints for preparing note cards:

1. Write a word or phrase that summarizes the information on the top left-hand corner of the note card.
2. Write the number from the bibliography card that lists the source of the information used on the top right-hand corner of the note card.
3. Write the information on the note cards in your own words (paraphrase). Write only one idea per note card. Do not write notes from two sources on the same card.
4. If using quoted material, write the material enclosed in quotation marks. Limit the use of direct quotes when taking notes.
5. At the bottom of every note card, write the page number of the source in which the information was found.*

Organic material in streams 2

Streams and rivers contain organic matter made by aquatic organisms. Sticks, pieces of fruit, leaves, and animal waste wash into rivers and streams from many places.

p. 98

*Adapted from *How To Write A Great Research Paper*, Incentive Publications, Nashville, TN.

Sample Note Sheet

Name ______________________________ Date ______________________________

Source ____

Title of Source: ____

Author's Name: ____

Publisher: ____

Copyright Year: ____

Place of Publication: ____

Page Numbers: ____

Title of Research: ____

Write your notes IN YOUR OWN WORDS:

____

____

____

____

____

____

____

____

____

____

____

____

____

If necessary, continue your notes on another sheet of paper.

Name ____________________

Practice Note Taking

Use your judgment in choosing the most important and least important statements. Read the article carefully, then answer the questions that follow.

Food and Game Fish

Fish is one of the most nourishing foods. The amount of protein found in fish is about the same as that found in meat. Every year, several million tons of tuna, cod, herring, and other ocean food fish are caught by commercial fishermen. There are also many inland waters where commercial fishing takes place. Salmon, trout, and perch are some types of freshwater food fish.

The business of fish farming is called aquaculture. Fish farms raise fish for food. In the United States salmon, catfish, and trout are raised on fish farms. In other countries in the world, fish and carp are raised in fish farms. Ponds are used by fish farmers for raising the fish. They use special feeding methods to grow fish larger and faster than they would grow in the wild.

Many people enjoy fishing for fun. They like to go after game fish. They include swordfish and marlin in the ocean and trout and bass in fresh water. Game fish are exciting to catch because of their size and fighting spirit.

1. What are two results of using special feeding methods in fish farming?

____

____

2. What is so nourishing about fish?

____

____

3. Name three types of fish raised on fish farms in the United States.

____

____

4. What is so exciting about catching game fish?

____

____

Practice Note Taking

When taking notes, begin by skimming the material in order to get a general idea of the content. When reading the material for the second time, read more carefully in order to find the main points and details. Instead of writing complete sentences, make brief notes.

On the right side of this page, take notes on the article below. Remember to use brief notes instead of complete sentences. Check the article for main ideas, cue words, and punctuation. Remember to use quotation marks for direct quotes.

The Mongolian Gerbil	Notes
There are approximately one hundred species of gerbils. They are found in the dry areas of Asia and Africa. The most well-known type is the Mongolian gerbil. It makes a good pet for the following reasons: its calm nature, its interesting behavior, and its curiosity. The Mongolian gerbil is approximately 8 inches long and weighs about 3 ounces. On the tip of its tail is a tuft of black hair. The Mongolian gerbil ranges in color from yellow to brown or gray. Its feet have strong, black or dark brown claws. The Mongolian who normally walks on four legs sometimes hops like a kangaroo, using only its hind legs. In the wild, these gerbils are found in parts of Russia and China as well as throughout parts of Mongolia. They live in groups which form colonies and they burrow in the ground for shelter. These gerbils are active during daylight hours as well as evening hours. Their main sources of food include seeds, roots, leaves, bulbs, and stems. Mongolian gerbils can reproduce when they are only ten to twelve weeks old. The female gerbil carries the unborn babies for twenty-four to twenty-six days. The female gerbil may produce as many as twelve babies at a time but normally produces an average of four.	

Chapter Eight

CREATING AN OUTLINE

Creating an Outline

Creating an outline will make writing a research paper easier. Think of an outline as the "writing plan." An outline helps the writer sort out the main ideas and the supporting facts. The main ideas and supporting facts were recorded on the note cards during the research phase of the project. The outline will help plan the best order for those ideas.

1. Write the title of the paper across the top of the page.
2. Place a Roman numeral and a period before each main topic.
3. When dividing the main topic into subtopics, be sure to place the "A" directly underneath the first letter of the first word of the main topic.
4. If a main topic is divided, it must have at least two subtopics.
5. If using words or phrases instead of complete sentences in the outline, do not place a period after a main topic or subtopic.
6. Always begin the main topic and subtopic with a capital letter and capitalize any proper nouns.
7. An outline should use parallel structure. In other words, the same kind of word or phrase should be used.

Incorrect Use: I. Living in Space
A. Providing for basic needs
B. Communication

The example is incorrect because it does not use parallel structure consistently. The topic is a phrase, the first subtopic is a phrase, and the second subtopic is a single word. The following example shows an outline correctly written in phrases.

Providing Medical Care

I. Elements of Medical Care
A. Diagnosis of Patients
B. Treatment of Patients
C. Prevention of Diseases
II. Provision of Medical Care
A. Care of Patients
B. Location of Medical Care
C. Quality Improvement of Medical Care
III. Careers in Medicine
A. Career as a Doctor
B. Career as a Nurse
C. Career as a Technician
IV. Problems in Medical Care

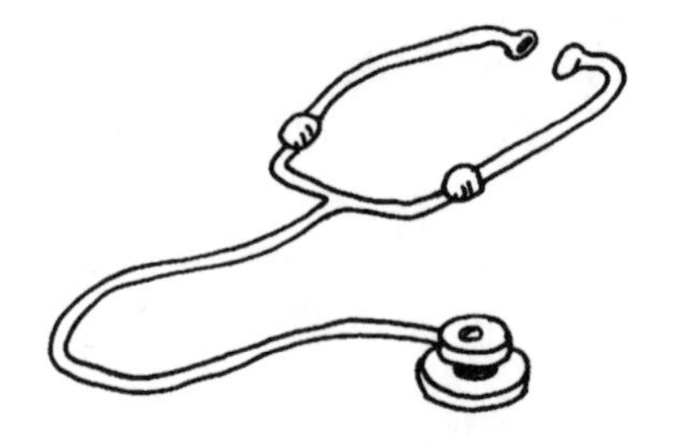

Outlining Practice

Read the following information, then complete the outline under the major headings on the following page.

Spiders and Their Webs

There are seven kinds of silk glands that a spider may have. No spider has all seven kinds. Every spider has at least three types of silk glands, and most have five. Each gland produces a different kind of silk. Spiders use each of these types of silk for a particular purpose.

Spiders use spinnerets to spin the silk. They work like the fingers of a human hand. Spiders can stretch out, pull back, and squeeze all of the spinnerets. Spiders can make a thick wide band or a very thin thread of silk by combining silk from different silk glands.

They may also create a sticky thread that looks like a beaded necklace. In order to do this, the spider pulls dry thread that is covered with sticky silk. It uses the claws on one of its hind legs, stretches the thread and then releases it with a snap. The results of this cause the liquid silk to form little beads along the thread. These beaded threads are used by the spider to trap flying or jumping insects.

Spiders rely on silk in a variety of ways. No matter where a spider goes, a silken thread is spun from behind, which is known as a dragline. The spider uses this dragline to escape from predators. While in its web, a spider can drop from the web and return to the web on the dragline. Spiders use different kinds of silk to create a nest for their home. Some nests are made in the ground and others are in the middle of their webs. Sometimes spiders use the silk to wrap their victims like mummies, so escape is impossible. Most female spiders wrap their eggs with a special kind of silk to create an egg sac.

The simplest type of web is a mixture of thread attached to a support, such as under the eaves of a house. Oftentimes cobwebs found in houses are webs that have collected dust. Some tangled webs have a tightly woven sheet of silk in the center. This sheet acts like an insect trap. Other tangled webs contain a band of dry and sticky silk.

Another type of spider web consists of flat sheets of silk between blades of grass or branches of trees. When a flying insect strikes the net, it lands in the sheet web. The spider quickly runs to the insect and pulls it through the webbing. This type of web lasts a long time because the spider repairs any damaged parts. Some sheet webs are created with two separate sheets. The spider hangs under the top sheet, while the bottom sheet protects the spider from attack below.

The most complicated of all webs is the round web. Round webs are found in open areas between tree branches or stems of flowers. From the center of the web, threads of dry silk extend like the spokes of a wheel. The spokes are connected with lines of sticky coiling silk that serve as a trap for insects. Spiders on these webs either wait in the center of the web or they hang on a trap line to wait for their prey.

Name ____________________

Outlining Practice

After reading the story on spiders, complete the following outline.

Spiders and Their Webs

I. Spiders' Silk

A. ____________________

1. ____________________

2. ____________________

B. ____________________

1. ____________________

2. ____________________

3. ____________________

4. ____________________

II. Web Types

A. ____________________

B. ____________________

C. ____________________

Name ______________________________

Outlining Practice

To further test outline knowledge, parts of two outlines are given below. The outlines are in scrambled order. For the first outline (on the left), the form is supplied. For the second outline, create the form from scratch.

Measuring of Time	Main Sequence Stars
Formation of Stars	Change and Death of Stars
Stars in the Universe	Distance of Stars
Mystery Stars	Binary Stars
Learning from the Stars	Measuring of Direction
Kinds of Stars	
Number of Stars	

Studying the Stars

I. ______________________________

A. ______________________

B. Size of Stars

C. ______________________

II. Use of the Stars

A. ______________________

B. ______________________

C. ______________________

III. ______________________________

A. ______________________

B. Variable Stars

C. ______________________

D. ______________________

IV. The Birth and Death of Stars

A. ______________________

B. ______________________

Suggestion: Put the Roman numerals first for each of the three main topics. Then leave spaces for the subtopics under each main topic.

Uses of Corn	Milling
Distilling	Sweet Corn
Flour Corn	Livestock Feed
Food for Humans	Flint Corn
Processing of Corn	Feed Manufacturing
Kinds of Corn	Dent Corn

Growing Corn

Chapter Nine

CONDUCTING EXPERIMENTS

Planning an Experiment

When planning an experiment, think about the topic. Can the topic question be answered by researching information only? If so, then it is material for a report, not for a science experiment that can be used for a science project. One topic that is considered for science fairs is "What are Gamma Rays?" This topic might make a good report; however, there is no experimentation needed to answer the question.

Here are some examples of questions that can be answered through experimentation:

- **Do Different Colored Gummy Bears Taste Different?**
- **Which Toothpaste Works Best?**
- **Does Fresh Water Hold Heat Longer Than Salt Water?**
- **What Are The Effects Of A Low-Fat Diet On Cholesterol?**

To understand what scientists do, complete experiments rather than reports.

Here is an example of the correct way to set up and conduct an experiment. This experiment involves testing the effect of practicing on the ability to jump higher. Make a prediction, the **hypothesis**, about what will happen.

Materials:

Pencil

Ruler

Calendar

Masking Tape

Data Table

Procedure:

Record your current vertical jump. (Take an average of six jumps.)
To perform a vertical jump: Stand flat-footed against the wall and mark the height of your fingertips. Then jump and record the height of your fingertips. The difference between the two heights is your vertical jump.

Perform a vertical jump every other day for two months. For practice, drop jump daily. Begin by standing on the first step of a set of stairs. Jump to the ground and back. The next time, jump from the ground to the second step and back. Finally, jump from the ground to the third step and back. Record the results of your vertical jumps for the two-month period.

Analysis of Data:

Use your data table to determine the results of your experimentation. Look at your hypothesis to decide if the results supported your predictions. Use the data table to create a graph, chart, or diagram, showing the results of your experimentation.

Conclusion:

Write a paragraph describing your results and the reason(s) for those results. This paragraph should include one or more sentences that either support or reject the hypothesis of the experiment. A successful science project will usually suggest further experiments that can be conducted based on the results. In most experiments, scientists have difficulties with the variables, gathering data, or other parts of the scientific method. Any problems experienced should be recorded in the conclusion section.

____

____

____

____

____

____

____

____

____

____

____

____

____

Name ______________________________

Making a Hypothesis

The best way to explain what will be learned from the scientific investigation is to write a question. The next step is to guess what will happen in the experiment. Scientists call this guess a *hypothesis*. A clearly written hypothesis answers the question and is brief and to the point. The following is an example:

Topic: Factors That Affect Tooth Decay

Question: Which liquid causes teeth to decay faster?

Hypothesis: Orange juice will cause a tooth to decay faster than other liquids.

Write a hypothesis for each of the following questions.

1. What are the effects of bleach and dye on hair?

   Hypothesis: ______________________________

2. Which type of food molds the fastest?

   Hypothesis: ______________________________

3. What are the effects of cola on teeth?

   Hypothesis: ______________________________

4. Does the use of computers improve student performance?

   Hypothesis: ______________________________

5. Does soil type change how well plants grow?

   Hypothesis: ______________________________

6. What factors affect the bounce of a dropped ball?

   Hypothesis: ______________________________

7. Which mouthwash kills the most microbes?

   Hypothesis: ______________________________

8. Which types of treats do dogs prefer?

   Hypothesis: ______________________________

Name ____

Experimental Studies

In experimental studies, examine all of the factors that might change an experiment. Alter certain conditions and then observe how they affect the experiment. The conditions that are altered are called variables. There are two types of variables, independent and dependent. An independent variable is one that is purposely changed before the experiment. A dependent variable is one that must be measured and recorded during the experiment.

In a **controlled** experiment, two groups may be needed: the experimental group in which only one variable is changed at a time; and the control group in which there are no variables. On the other hand, the science project may not require a control group.

Two hypotheses are listed below. For each hypothesis, name the variable that would be changed to help solve the hypothesis. Then list the controlled variables that would stay the same for every test. The first hypothesis has been completed as an example to follow.

Hypothesis I: *"Wrap-It" Plastic Wrap will be the strongest.*

Independent Variable: different brands of plastic wrap

Dependent Variable: the strength of the different plastic wraps

Controls: same size test sheet, same weight, same amount of time

Hypothesis II: *"Orange Juice will cause a tooth to decay faster than other liquids."*

Independent Variable: ____

____

Dependent Variable: ____

Controls: ____

____

____

Name ______________________________

Experimental Design Practice

Use the experiments described on pages 51–52 or one that the teacher assigns to complete the following form:

☐ Problem

____

____

☐ Hypothesis

____

____

☐ Materials

____

____

☐ Independent Variable(s)

____

____

☐ Dependent Variable

____

____

☐ Control

____

____

Chapter Ten

RECORDING LOG BOOK RESULTS

Setting Up Your Log Book

Give careful thought to setting up a log book. While conducting research and experimentation, keep detailed notes about each and every experiment, measurement, and observation in a stitched or glue-bound log book. Log book entries should be dated and written in ink only.

Remember to change only one variable at a time when experimenting, and be sure to include control experiments in which none of the variables are changed. Be sure to also include sufficient numbers of test subjects in both the control and the experimental groups. Plan on doing the experiment several times. Please note that things rarely work the first time the experiment is executed.

As experimentation proceeds, all of the observations and any other ideas related to your experiment should be written in the log book. There are various ways to record information into the log book; however, it is always smart to date the entry at the top of each page. Moreover, this idea will help keep the results of the experiments organized when it is time to write the research paper.

The following is a page-by-page recommendation for setting up your log book:

Page 1

Title Page

Title of Science Project

Question

Student's Name

Student's Address

School Name

School Address

Grade

(On Bottom of Page)

Research Start Date

Research End Date

Experiment Start Date

Experiment End Date

Page 2

Timeline Due Dates

	Date Due	Date Completed
a) Topic Question Due for Approval	______	______
b) Research Note Check	______	______
c) Hypothesis Due	______	______
d) Experimental Design	______	______
e) Experiment	______	______
f) Observations and Analysis	______	______
g) Conclusion and Abstract Sheet	______	______
h) Science Research Paper with Abstract and Bibliography	______	______
i) Backboard Completed		
j) Log Book with Research Notes, Experimental Design, Observations, Analysis, & Conclusions	______	______

Page 3

Table of Contents

	Page(s)
Research Notes	______
Hypothesis	______
Experimental Design	______
Experimental Observations	______
Analysis (Hand-Drawn Charts & Graphs)	______
Conclusion	______
Other Information	______

The following are examples of log book entries:

TITLE PAGE

Boiling Liquids

Which substance reaches the boiling point the fastest?

Manuel Rodriguez
2453 Henderson Road
Decatur, Georgia 30003

Henderson Middle School
3830 Georgia Mill Road
Chamblee, Georgia 30134

Grade 8

Research started October 1, 2001
Research ended November 4, 2001
Experiment started November 8, 2001
Experiment ended December 20, 2001

Time Line Due Dates

	Date Due	Date Completed
a) Topic question due for approval	9/22/01	9/22/01
b) Research note check	11/5/01	11/1/01
c) Hypothesis due	11/8/01	11/3/01
d) Experimental design	11/15/01	11/15/01
e) Experiment	12/20/01	12/20/01
f) Observations and Analysis	12/21/01	12/21/01
g) Conclusion and Abstract	1/12/02	1/10/02
h) Science Research Paper	2/14/02	2/14/02
i) Backboard Completed	2/28/02	2/20/02
j) Log Book due	3/1/02	3/1/02

Table of Contents

Experimental Design p. 7

Materials:
5 cooking pots (2 quarts each)
1 cup BBQ sauce
1 cup water with 1/4 tsp. salt
1 cup water with 1/4 tsp. cooking oil
1 cup water
1 cup milk
stove
stop watch

Procedures:
Pour each of the liquids in a pot. Put pot 1 on stove and turn burner on to medium. Start stop watch. Write down information in log book. When first liquid boils, record time. Follow the same procedure for each of the liquids.
Repeat this procedure each day of the experiment.

Observations p.9

12-20-01

Milk put in the pan, heat turned on at 5:00 pm
Milk began to boil after 9 minutes and 9 seconds.
Water put in the pan, heat turned on at 5:12 pm
Water began to boil after 5 minutes and 28 seconds.
BBQ sauce put in the pan, and heat turned on 5:20 pm.
BBQ sauce began to boil after 3 minutes and 48 seconds.
Water with oil put in the pan, and heat turned on at 5:30 pm
Water with oil began to boil after 5 minutes and 19 seconds.
Water with salt put in pan, and heat turned on at 5:45 pm
Water with salt began to boil after 4 minutes and 19 seconds.

Analysis page 21

Liquid:	Trial 1	2	3	4	5
milk	9m 9s	9m 12s	9m 10s	9m 12s	9m 8s
water	5m 28s	5m 28s	5m 30s	5m 31s	5m 28s
BBQ sauce	3m 48s	4m 2s	3m 50s	3m 51s	3m 50s
water with oil	5m 19s	5m 18s	5m 17s	5m 18s	5m 19s
water with salt	4m 19s	4m 25s	4m 19s	4m 19s	4m 19s

time = time liquid took to boil

m = minutes

s = seconds

Chapter Eleven

WRITING THE RESEARCH PAPER

Guidelines for the Research Paper

Upon the completion of experimentation, it is time to write the first draft of the research paper. When starting a first draft, concentrate only on putting the main ideas on paper. Do not be concerned with punctuation, grammar, or spelling. The following evaluation guidelines will help as the draft is written.

Title Page	Include project title, name, address, school, and grade.
Table of Contents	Number each section when writing is complete.
Introduction	The introduction should explain the background information concerning the topic and the reasons for the choice of study. Refer to previous research, as well as the project's experiments. Establish a strong rationale for the study by emphasizing unresolved issues or questions. Conclude by stating the research hypothesis.
Materials & Procedures	Describe in detail the methodology used to derive the data and observations. Use photographs and drawings of the equipment to describe your experiment further. Include a precise description of the sample, any apparatus that was constructed or modified for the study, and methods of data collection.
Results	Present the data collected in the experiment in tables and graphs. Summarize the data in narrative form. Include statistical analysis of the data. Do not include raw data. Include only information collected during the current year's study.
Discussion	The results and conclusion should flow smoothly and logically from the data. Be thorough. Compare results with theoretical values, published data, commonly held beliefs, and/or expected results. A complete paper should include a discussion of possible errors or problems experienced.
Conclusion	Briefly summarize the results. Discuss if the data supported the hypothesis and what the next steps in experimentation may be.

Acknowledgements and Credits — Credit any assistance received from mentors, parents, teachers, and other sources.

Bibliography — The reference list should include any material that is found in outside sources (i.e, books, encyclopedias, websites, papers, journal articles, and communications cited in the paper). Follow the prescribed bibliographic recommendations in this book.

Appendix — Include critical information that is too lengthy for the main section of the paper, such as raw data, additional tables and graphs, copies of surveys and tests, and diagrams of specialized equipment.

Adapted from International Rules for Precollege Science Research: Guidelines for Science and Engineering Science Fairs, 2000–2001.

Here are examples of an introductory paragraph and conclusion:

Introductory Paragraph

It is a well known fact that water boils at 212°F at sea level. While watching my mother prepare dinner, I observed water boiling which caused me to wonder about other substances and their boiling points. I wondered if some substances, such as BBQ sauce, milk, water with salt, water with oil, and soup, would come to a boil faster than others. I believe the hardest decision to make was choosing which substances to use in my experiment. I thought this project was going to be an easy one; however, it was actually much more difficult than I possibly imagined. My hypothesis was that water will come to a boil faster than other substances.

Conclusion

By conducting my experimentation, I discovered that my hypothesis was wrong. It does not matter how light the color of the bulb may be. Light quality refers to the color or wavelength reaching the plant surface. Sunlight can be broken up by a prism into respective colors of red, orange, yellow, green, blue, indigo, and violet. On a rainy day, raindrops act as tiny prisms and break the sunlight into these colors, producing a rainbow. Red and blue have the greatest effect on plant growth. Green light is least effective to plants as they reflect green light and absorb none. Blue light is primarily responsible for leaf growth. Red light, when combined with blue light, encourages flowering in plants. During my research, I learned why plants need light. Light helps provide the energy plants need to make the food required for them to grow and flower.

Writing the Abstract

Abstracts, which are concise summaries of articles or books, routinely precede articles in journals and in certain periodical or bibliographic guides. Abstracts can help a reader decide whether to read the entire work. In the case of your science research project, you may be required to write an abstract.

The following rules are based on those from the International Rules for Precollege Science Research: Guidelines for Science Fairs, sponsored by Science Services, Inc., Washington, D.C.

- The abstract must be typed.
- Using all capitals, type the title, student name, district fair, and category.
- The abstract should be 250 words or less.
- The abstract ***should*** include the following:
  a) purpose of the experiment
  b) procedures used
  c) data
  d) conclusion
  e) any possible research application
  f) minimal reference to previous work
- The abstract ***should not*** include
  a) acknowledgements
  b) work or procedures completed by someone other than the student.

The following is an example of an abstract:

TITLE: *HOW HYDROGEN CAN BE USED TO PRODUCE LARGE AMOUNTS OF ENERGY*

NAME: IANKO P. CHTEREV

REGIONAL FAIR: DEKALB/ROCKDALE SCIENCE & MATHEMATICS FAIR

CATEGORY: PHYSICAL SCIENCE

The purpose of this experiment was to find how water molecules could be broken up into hydrogen and oxygen gases. The procedures of the electrolysis lab I performed are as follows:

- Fill a large plastic container with water.
- Fill two smaller containers with equal capacity.
- Cover the opening and flip the containers upside down into the larger container of water.
- Put the two graphite electrodes into the small containers and connect to the copper wire.
- Pour in a tablespoon of baking soda.
- Connect a 12v DC current (0.5 amps) low power source.

After the experiment has been performed, hydrogen begins to form at the negative electrode, and oxygen formed on the positive. For a conversion device I constructed my own paper model, with a blade driven by an air current from a hair dryer. My hypothesis was correct. This experimental design may be constructed with more enhanced material for better results. A turbine may be rotated by the explosion created by the hydrogen and oxygen to drive a generator.

Centered and typed

Table of Contents

Notice all required parts are included.

Note each section indicates the beginning page.

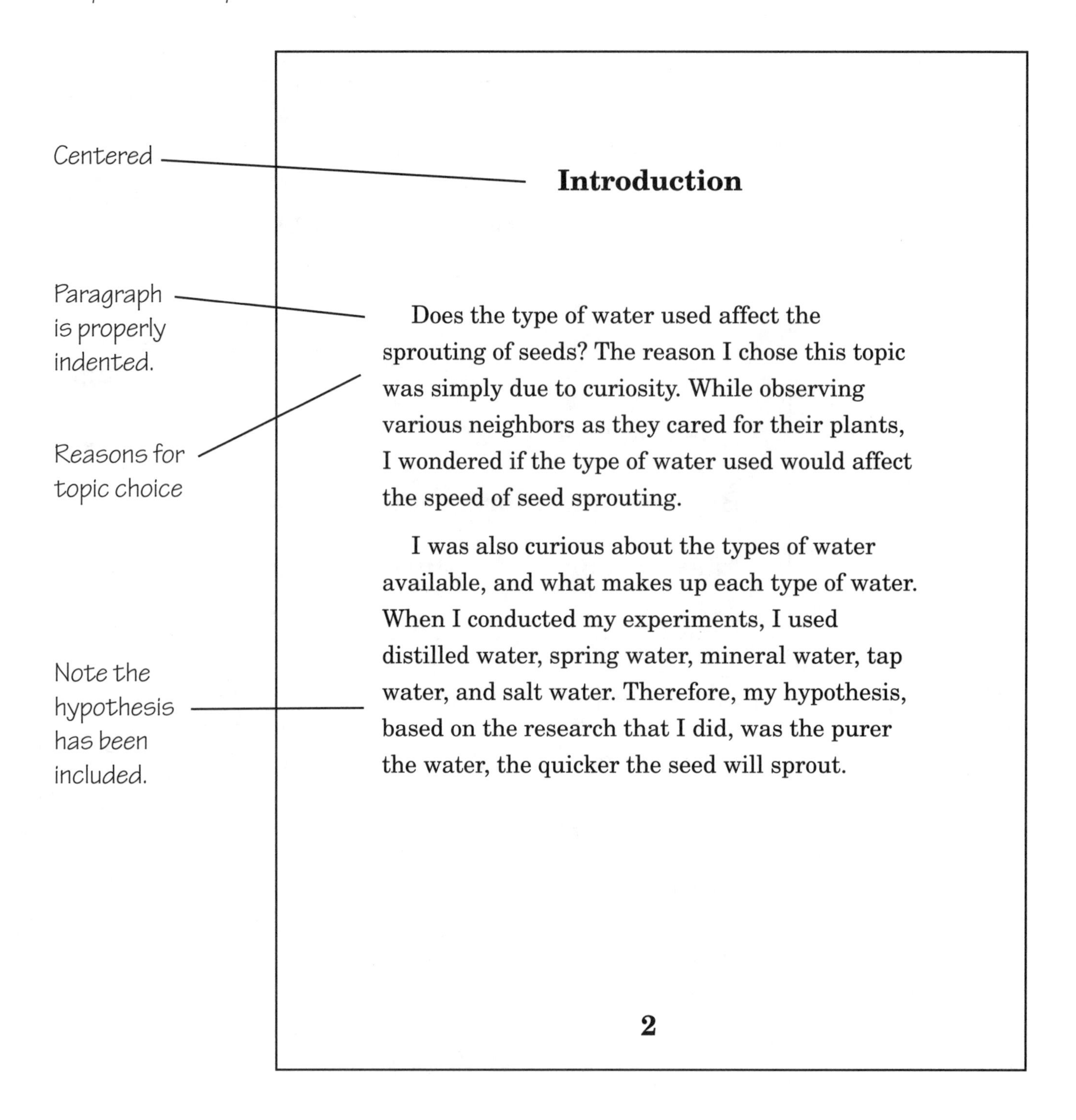
Centered
Paragraph is properly indented.
Reasons for topic choice
Note the hypothesis has been included.
Introduction
Does the type of water used affect the sprouting of seeds? The reason I chose this topic was simply due to curiosity. While observing various neighbors as they cared for their plants, I wondered if the type of water used would affect the speed of seed sprouting.
I was also curious about the types of water available, and what makes up each type of water. When I conducted my experiments, I used distilled water, spring water, mineral water, tap water, and salt water. Therefore, my hypothesis, based on the research that I did, was the purer the water, the quicker the seed will sprout.
2

Section centered

Paragraph indented

References to previous experiments used

Background Information

Water is the common name for the liquid state of the hydrogen-oxygen compound, H_2O. Ancient philosophers regarded water as a basic element that demonstrated the typical liquid. It was not until 1783 that a French chemist proved that water was actually a compound of oxygen and hydrogen. In 1804, another French chemist and a German naturalist demonstrated that water was made of two volumes of hydrogen and one volume of oxygen.

Pure water is an odorless, tasteless liquid. It has a bluish tint, which may be detected only in deep layers. The freezing point of water is 0°C (32°F), and its boiling point is 100°C (212°F). Water attains its maximum density at a temperature of 4°C (39°F), and expands upon freezing. Like most other liquids, water can exist in a super-cooled state; that is, it can stay in liquid form even though its temperature is below freezing.

Water is one of the best known ionizing agents. This is true because most substances are somewhat soluble in water. Water is often called the universal solvent. Water combines with certain salts to form hydrates. it reacts with metal oxides to form acids. Protoplast, the basic material of living cells, consists of a solution in water of fats, carbohydrates, proteins, salts, and similar chemicals. Water acts as a solvent, transporting, combining, and chemically breaking down these substances. Because of its tendency to dissolve many materials in large amounts, rarely in nature can pure water be found.

3

Note that references are made to the differences in types of water.

During condensation and precipitation, rain or snow absorbs different amounts of carbon dioxide and other gases from the atmosphere. Also, precipitation carries radioactive fallout to the earth's surface. As the water moves on and through the earth's crust, it reacts with minerals in the soil and rocks. Most of the dissolved materials in surface and groundwater are sulfates, chlorides, bicarbonates of sodium and potassium, and the oxides of calcium and magnesium. Surface waters may also contain sewage and industrial wastes. Groundwater may contain large amounts of nitrogen compounds and chlorides from human and animal wastes. Almost all supplies of natural drinking water contain fluorides in differing amounts. Suspended and dissolved impurities in naturally occurring water make it unsuitable for many things. There are many steps that are followed to cleanse water before it comes through the tap.

Mineral water is water that comes from a geologically and physically protected underground water source. Mineral water must contain minerals and/or other trace elements that make it distinguishable from other kinds of water.

Spring water is considered to be water that flows naturally from an underground source to the surface of the earth. It must be collected directly from the spring or from a bore hole is next to the place where the water comes naturally to the surface.

4

Section centered

Materials and Procedures

Materials:

Flush to left margin

Five small paper pots
Five Kentucky Long Bean seeds
10 cups of potting soil
One gallon each of distilled water, spring water,
mineral water, tap water, and salt water
One large tray

Procedures:

Note the methodology used in experimentation.

1. Take each of the pots and fill each one $^2/_3$ full of potting soil. For easy reference, label each pot with the type of water to be used.
2. In each pot, place one bean seed in the soil. Cover the seed with one inch of soil.
3. Take $^1/_3$ cup each of tap water, salt water, distilled water, spring water, and mineral water; then pour it carefully into the correctly labeled pot.
4. Place all of the pots in the tray. Then place the tray in a sunny area.

Note the method of data collection.

5. Record the date and time.
6. Check the seeds every day for signs of sprouting. Record date, time, and any noticeable changes.
7. Repeat step #3 every other day, recording the date and time.
8. When the experimentation has been completed, repeat the entire experiment for accuracy.

7

Section centered

Results

Observe the results shown in table format.

Types of Water	Results
Tap Water	Sprouted second
Distilled Water	Sprouted first
Spring Water	Sprouted third
Salt Water	Did not sprout
Mineral Water	Did not sprout

Note narrative form for data summarization.

On the sixth day of watering, the first sprout, using the distilled water, came up. Actually, the little plant looked normal. Later the same day, the tap water seed sprouted. By observing the height of the sprouts, it was obvious which one sprouted first. The third seed to sprout was the one on which spring water was used. The seeds which were given salt water and mineral water never germinated.

8

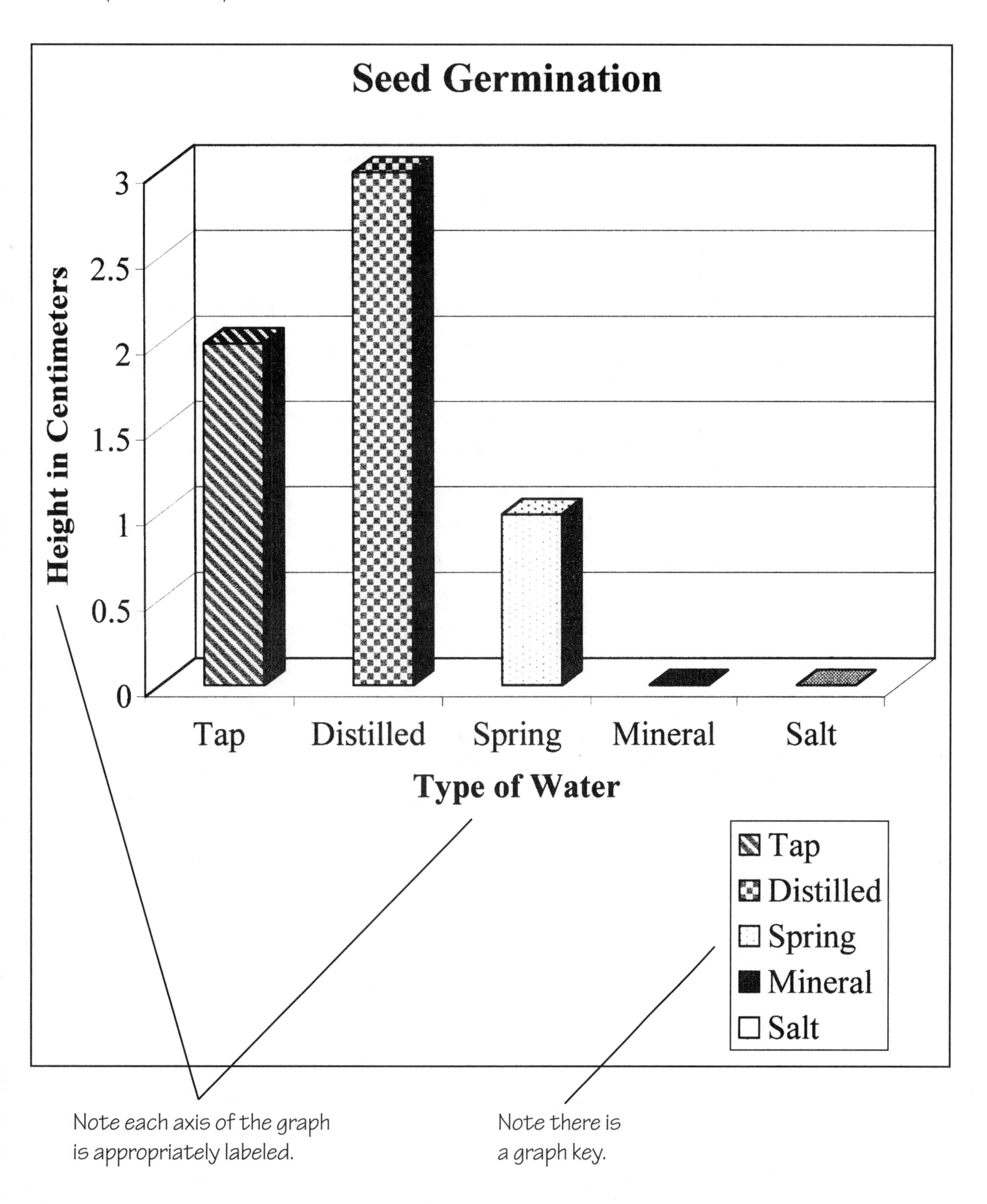
Seed Germination
Height in Centimeters
3
2.5
2
1.5
1
0.5
0
Tap
Distilled
Spring
Mineral
Salt
Type of Water
Tap
Distilled
Spring
Mineral
Salt
Note each axis of the graph is appropriately labeled.
Note there is a graph key.

Section centered

Discussion

What do those results actually mean? From my experiment, the distilled water caused the sprout to grow the fastest. Does that mean that everyone should use distilled water when watering their plants? I do not think so. Distilled water is water that was filtered by steam distillation. Distillation is based on the fact that the vapor of a boiling mixture will be richer in the components that have lower boiling points; therefore, when this vapor is cooled and condensed, the condensed vapor will contain more volatile components. At the same time, the original mixture will contain more of the less volatile material. Distillation columns are designed to achieve this separation efficiently. Since the steam filtering was used in distilled water, which is similar to the natural water cycle, the sprout grew faster. Perhaps another possibility is that the steam filtering removed more of the particles, and that caused it to grow faster.

Note the results included.

The seeds that were given tap water and spring water also grew. Tap water contains fluorides in varying amounts. Other minerals, such as calcium, magnesium, and aluminum, can also be found in tap water. Almost all other impurities are removed. On

10

the other hand, spring water comes directly from a natural spring and does not necessitate water purification. Because of the fact that spring water and tap water share some mineral content, the seeds sprouted, but at a slower rate than the one given distilled water.

The seeds which were given salt water and mineral water did not sprout at all. The salt was probably too acidic for the bean seed. The sprout which was given mineral water probably did not germinate because of the water's carbonation. Mineral water contains minerals and/or trace elements that make it distinguishable from other types of water. Because of the greater mineral content, the seed did not germinate.

Experimentation data included

The seed which received distilled water grew to a height of three centimeters. The seed which received the tap water grew to a height of two centimeters. The third seed, the one given spring water, grew only one centimeter in height.

Discussion of possible problems

My experiment was controlled with the type of water being the only manipulative variable. Each seed received the same amount of sunlight and water. In addition, each seed was planted in the same size pot with equal amounts of soil. When I repeated the experiment, the results were the same. Both experiments proceeded smoothly with no unexpected problems.

11

Section centered

Conclusion

Note the summary of the results.

To summarize my results, three out of five bean seeds sprouted. The three were given tap water, spring water, and distilled water. In my experiment, the sprout which grew the fastest was the one which received the distilled water. It grew to a height of three centimeters. The seed which was given tap water grew two centimeters while the seed which received spring water grew to a height of one centimeter. Neither of the seeds that received salt water or mineral water grew. I believe this was due to the acidity of the salt water and the carbonation found in the mineral water.

Note the hypothesis was supported.

Through my research, I learned that distilled water is the purest of the water I used. Thus, I created a hypothesis stating that if the water is purer then the sprout will grow faster. The results of my experiment proved my hypothesis correct.

Note the next steps in continued experimentation.

If I attempted this experiment again, I might include artesian water, sparkling water, and well water.

12

Section centered

Acknowledgements

I would like to acknowledge the assistance of the following persons:

Elizabeth Thomas (my mother) for helping me purchase the supplies for my experiment and helping me select the type of seeds.

Alexander Thomas (my father) for buying my display board, paper, and other supplies.

Mrs. Mott (my teacher) for putting me on this long but interesting search, during which I learned a great deal.

Mrs. Jones (media specialist) for helping me with my research.

Note the credit given to parents, teachers, and other sources.

13

Section centered

Bibliography

Entries in alphabetical order.

Note the correct use of CD-ROM.

"Mineral Water." *Microsoft Encarta Online.* 2000. Microsoft Corporation. 27 November 2000.

"Plant." *Microsoft Encarta.* CD-ROM. Funk & Wagnall Corporation. 1994.

Skelsey, Alice. *Growing Up Green.* New York: Workman Publishing Company, 1973.

"Spring (water)." *Microsoft Encarta Online.* 2000. Microsoft Corporation. 7 December 2000.

"Tropism." *Microsoft Encarta.* CD-ROM. Funk & Wagnall Corporation. 1994.

"Water." *Microsoft Encarta.* CD-ROM. Funk & Wagnall Corporation. 1994.

14

PREPARING THE BACKBOARD

How To Begin a Backboard

1. Begin early gathering materials for the backboard. Save everything: copies of every letter written requesting information about your topic; magazine articles; newspaper articles; e-mails; photographs; pamphlets. Use a basket, drawer, or box to collect and save these items. Remember: Never discard anything until the project is complete.
2. Buy or build the backboard. (The backboards may be purchased from the local office supply or school supply store.) If student is making her backboard, she may purchase supplies from the local hardware store.
3. Backboards may be painted, covered with fabric or paper, or purchased in various colors.
4. Create a drawing of the backboard plan. Be sure to include the required parts of a backboard (see example on page 99). Try several sketches or plans and choose the one that best suits the purpose. Keep in mind that an orderly arrangement will bring unity to the work, and that a preliminary sketch will help work out problems on paper.
5. If required, submit the final drawing to the teacher for approval.
6. Once approved, use the plan to lay out the letters and other items gathered on the backboard. Be sure to leave neat margins and good spacing for your letters.
7. Ask someone to check the lettering for correct spelling! Glue the letters and other documentation to the backboard.

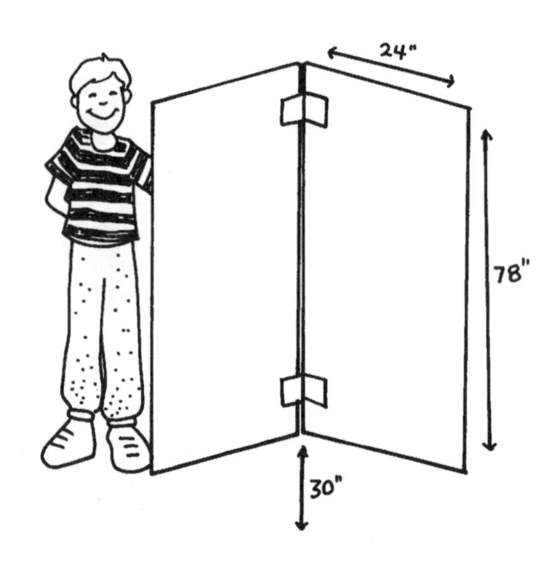

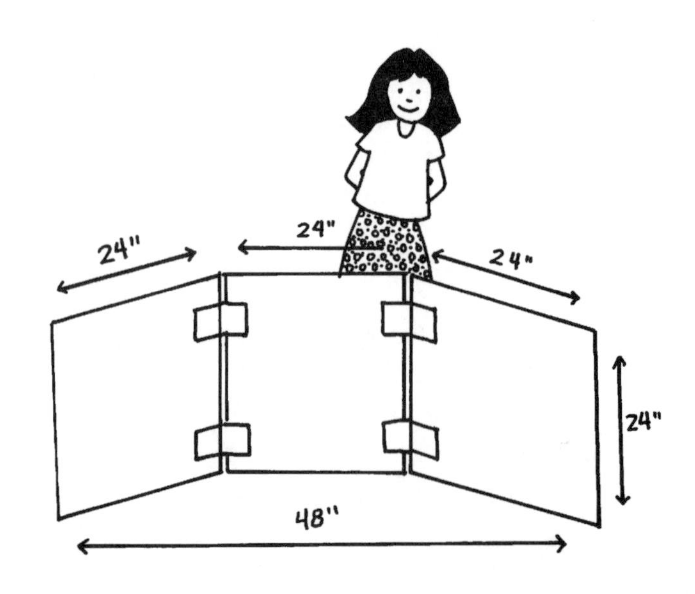

What Type of Backboard Should be Used?

The backboard should be made of sturdy materials, such as plywood, pegboard, cardboard, or another material. Commercially prepared foam core or cardboard backboards (pre-folded for easy use) can be found at art, office, or school supply stores. The backboard should be no larger than 48" in width, 78" in height, and 30" in depth. If desired, headers are also available. See the illustrations below for the correct use of a backboard.

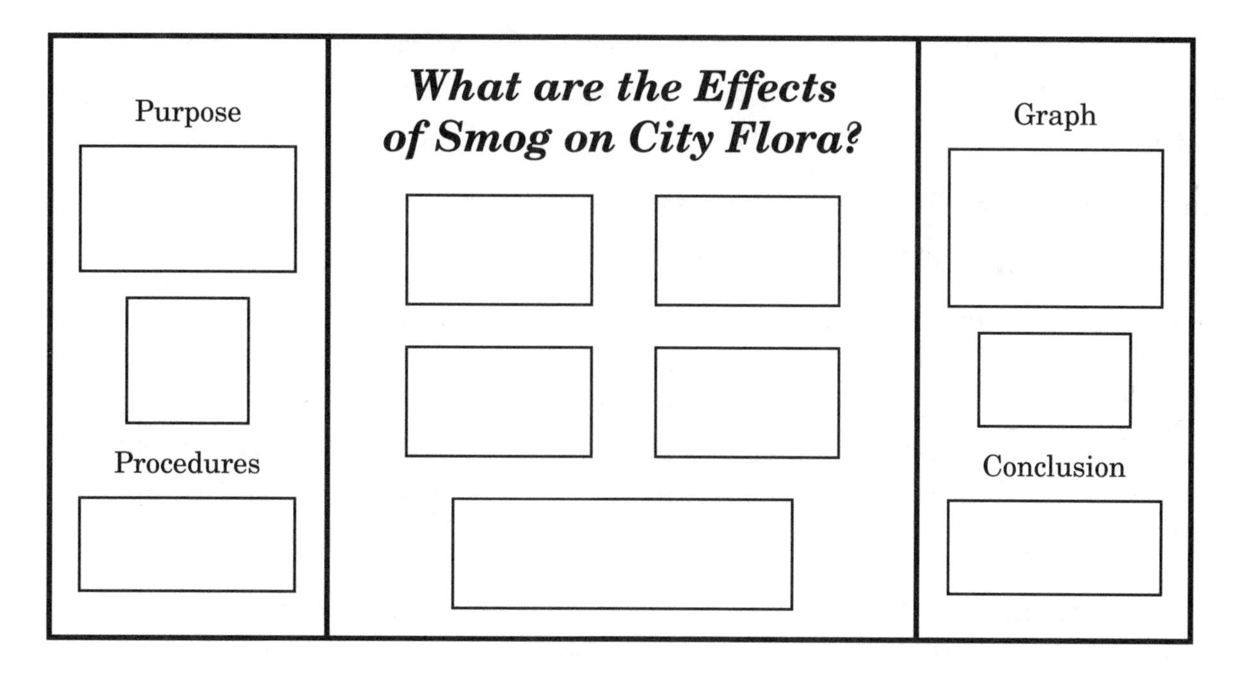

Advantages to Covering the Backboard

The color of the backboard should be part of the overall color scheme and should help reinforce the topic. A covered board should not fight the surface of the display board itself. For example, the grain of the wood, the texture of the circles in the pegboard, or the lines in the cardboard may compete with the design for attention. The background should be a part of the design and not something that works against it. Remember: A covered board should help to bring unity to the display.

Materials for Covering the Backboard

Painting the backboard will work well, especially on plywood. Make sure the paint is not too thin or watery. Felt or fabric that is not too thin can be used to cover your backboard. If you prefer, art craft paper may also be used to cover a backboard. A variety of colors is usually available. Finally, why not consider using a colorful border for the backboard? These borders are available in a wide variety of designs at the local art, office, or school supply store.

Decorating the Backboard

The materials for the backboard will depend on what is being illustrated. For example, use something as different as a fishing net if your topic calls for it. Try to be creative and use materials that will catch the eye of an audience and support the topic.

Design Elements

What design elements will make the backboard more attractive? An exceptional backboard, a work of art in itself, reflects good composition and an orderly arrangement. The following principles of design will help to create good composition:

Center of Interest: Is there something that catches the eye? A center of interest draws a viewer's attention.

Color Scheme: The use of a color scheme will help organize the backboard. The colors chosen may reflect the topic. For example, red, white and blue for a political theme; pastels for a feminine issue; black and yellow for a strong visual clarity; shades of blue for a marine topic; or black or white (with another color) always makes a strong statement.

Contrast: Is there enough of a difference between the chosen colors to make for easy reading? You do not want your work to fade into the background.

Balance: Check to see that the overall design is carried throughout the backboard. Try to make groups of items evenly distributed so that harmony is achieved.

Variety: Are the graphs, charts, maps, diagrams, timelines, or pictures interesting to the viewer?

Rhythm: An orderly progression is important to good composition. Since people read from left to right, it is advisable to place the purpose to the left of the board and to end with the conclusion on the right. Give the backboard a sense of order, and it will be more easily understood and read by the viewer.

Unity: Does the backboard work with all the parts coming together as a whole? A backboard will achieve unity if all the parts are necessary. Do not overdo your project! Make the work clear and concise.

Avoiding Backboard Pitfalls

1. Avoid using correction fluid because it draws attention to the mistake.
2. Use spray fixatives in a well-vented area. White glue will wrinkle the paper and once it is used, it has "no give" for re-positioning letters or pictures.
3. Use straight pins to place materials prior to gluing. Items can still be rearranged, but the pins will avoid unwanted movement.
4. Pin a piece of yarn with the ends at equal distances from the top of the backboard to use as a guideline for placing letters. Use a kneaded eraser to clean up drawn guidelines because kneaded erasers will not leave smears.
5. Take time to cut out pictures and graphs evenly. Ragged edges will draw attention.
6. For a framed look, use construction paper or colored paper to mat the pictures and graphs.
7. Use a decorative border of some kind, either handmade or purchased.
8. Rubber cement is a terrific adhesive, but it must be used in a vented area. If some of the rubber cement shows on the front of the backboard, let it dry and rub it into little balls for easy cleanup.
9. Never mark on uncovered foam-board. It is possible to erase the lead marking, but an impression will be left.

Chapter Fifteen

BACKBOARD PROJECT EXAMPLES

Physics Project Example

The following is an example of a Physics Science Project:

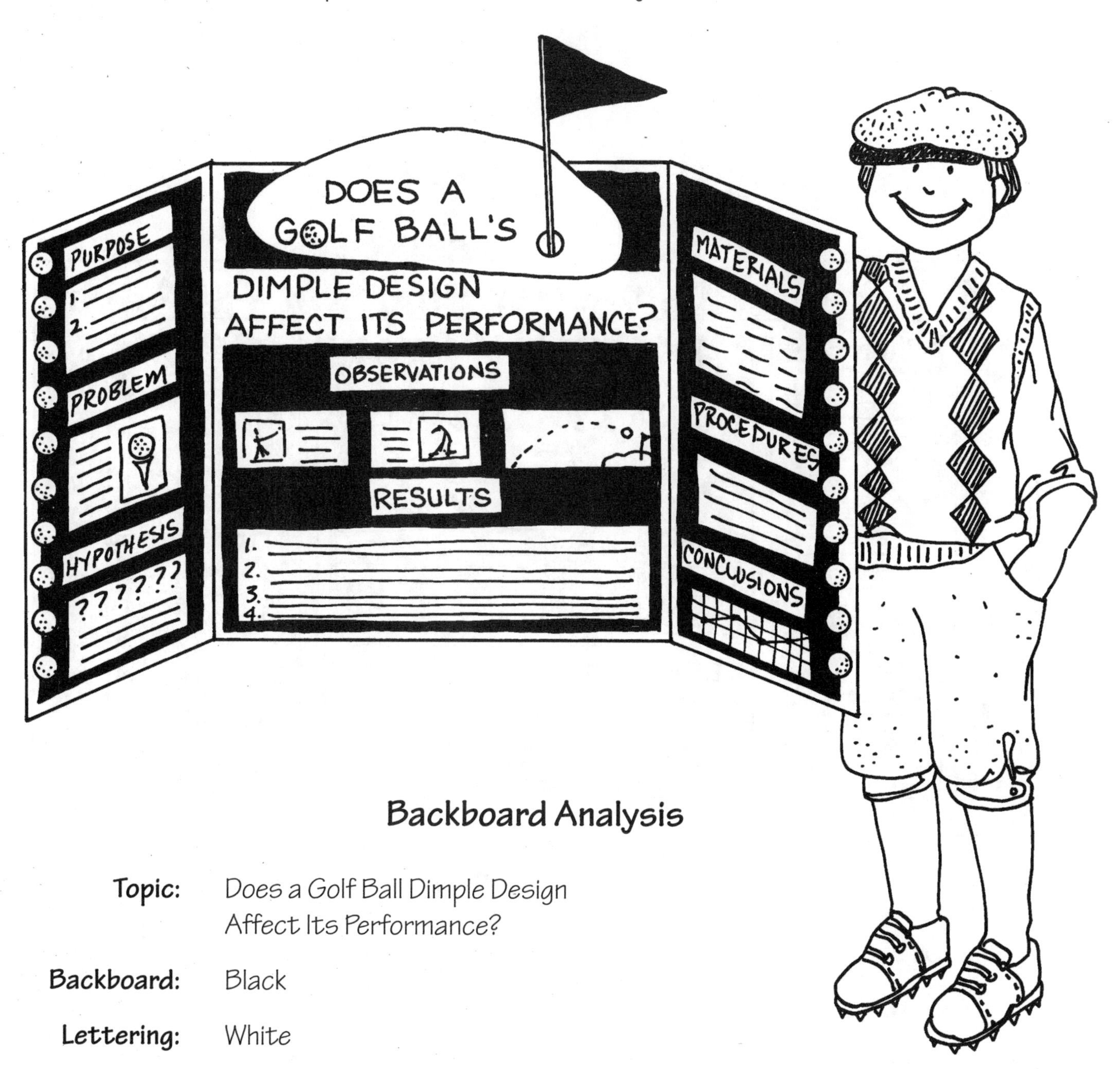

Backboard Analysis

Topic: Does a Golf Ball Dimple Design Affect Its Performance?

Backboard: Black

Lettering: White

Border: Golf balls along the sides only

Mats: Photos, graphs, labels, and charts are matted on green construction paper.

Labels: Purpose, Hypothesis, Problem, Observations, Results, Materials, Procedures, Conclusion

Chemistry Project Example

The following is an example of a Chemistry Science Project:

Backboard Analysis

Topic: How Can Hydrogen Be Used to Produce Energy?

Backboard: Blue

Lettering: Yellow

Border: White Scalloped Border with Blue Raindrops

Mats: Photos, graphs, labels, and charts are matted on yellow construction paper.

Labels: Purpose, Hypothesis, Problem, Observations, Results, Materials, Procedures, Conclusion

Medicine and Health Project Example

The following is an example of a Medicine and Health Project:

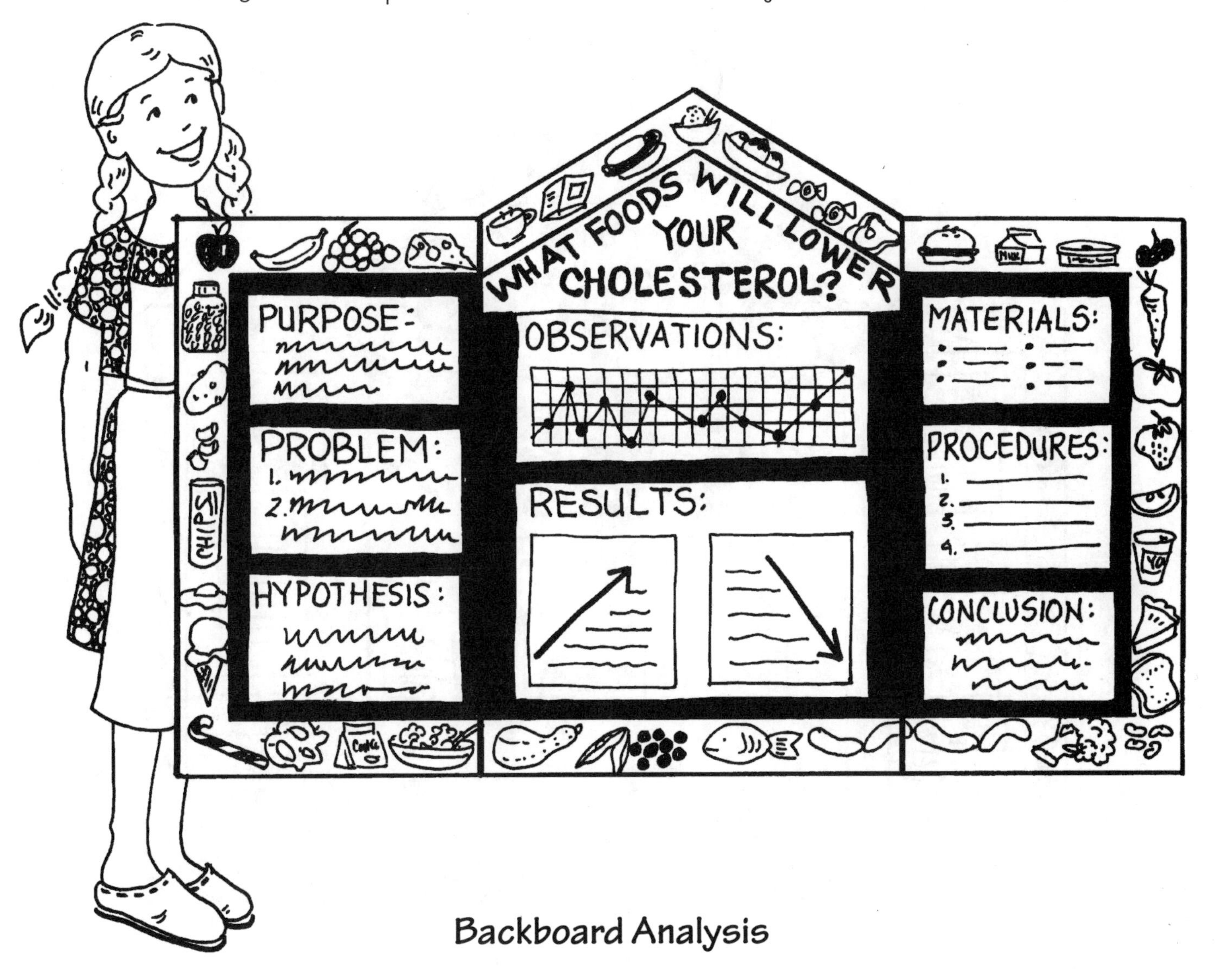

Backboard Analysis

Topic: What Foods Will Lower Your Cholesterol?

Backboard: Black

Lettering: Red

Border: White Border with Fruits and Vegetables

Mats: Photos, graphs, labels, and charts are matted on red construction paper.

Labels: Purpose, Hypothesis, Problem, Observations, Results, Materials, Procedures, Conclusion

Microbiology Project Example

The following is an example of a Microbiology Science Project:

Backboard Analysis

Topic: Which Mouthwash Kills the Most Microbes?

Backboard: Green

Lettering: Yellow

Border: Yellow Border with Pictures of Germs

Mats: Photos, graphs, labels, and charts are matted on white construction paper.

Labels: Purpose, Hypothesis, Problem, Observations, Results, Materials, Procedures, Conclusion

Botany Project Example

The following is an example of a Botany Science Project:

Backboard Analysis

Topic: Under What Color Light Do Plants Grow Best?

Backboard: White

Lettering: Green

Border: Scalloped Border with green leaves in the corners

Mats: Photos, graphs, labels, and charts are matted on black construction paper.

Labels: Purpose, Hypothesis, Problem, Observations, Results, Materials, Procedures, Conclusion

APPENDIX

Sample Letter to Parents

Date: ____________________

Dear Parent/Guardian:

____ *(Name of school)* Science Fair preparations are now underway. Your child received information today which describes the requirements, due dates, and format for the project. Participation in the Science Fair is optional; however, all students are required to complete the experimentation. A research paper and log book are also required. If your child wishes to compete in the Science Fair, a backboard must be included.

Please review this information with your child as soon as possible. The information was discussed in class. Your child will need your support and guidance in selecting a topic and locating information. However, in order for your child to have a successful project, it must represent his/her work, not that of a parent or expert.

A calendar is attached which includes the due dates for each aspect of the project (note-taking, an outline, an abstract, a research paper, and a bibliography). May we suggest a pocket folder for use in organizing all information and research? Note cards are suggested for taking notes. Your child may request that you proofread his/her paper for spelling and grammatical errors.

Your cooperation and support are appreciated in this valuable learning experience. When you and your child have reviewed this information, please sign the bottom portion and return it. Thank you.

Sincerely,

- -

Dear _________________________,

I have reviewed the Science Fair Project information

with my child, ____ *(child's name)*.

____________________ ____

Date *Parent/Guardian Signature*

Tips For Parents/Guardians

1. Review all information regarding the science project with your child. If you have any questions, contact the teacher who distributed the information.

2. Help your child choose a topic and be supportive of his or her final decision.

3. Allow your child time for thinking, exploring, and preparing his or her project.

4. Help your child by doing the following:

   - Driving him or her to the library.
   - Helping to arrange interviews.
   - Providing suggestions as to sources of information.
   - Proofreading and revising letters requesting information and/or materials.
   - Gathering printed materials related to his or her project.
   - Making suggestions for backboard design improvement.

   Remember: *Assist child in the completion of his or her science project. The operative word is assist. If the science project is to be a true learning experience for the child, it is imperative that the work be completed by the child.*

5. Proofread all material for grammatical correctness and content.

6. Be aware that your child may need assistance in transporting the project to and from school.

7. Show your support by going to the school, city, or county science fair.

8. Encourage your child to meet all deadlines that are set by the science teacher. Use a calendar to mark important dates.

9. Stress the value of thanking all individuals who have given any assistance or guidance in their scientific research and backboard production.

Sample Letter to Students

Date: ____________________

Dear Student:

The information concerning the requirements, due dates, and format of the ______________ (name of school) Science Fair are being distributed and discussed today. The participation in the science fair includes completing experimentation, completing a logbook, and creating a backboard. The research paper and project will be included as part of your science grade.

Review the information in this packet with your parent/guardian. You may need their help and support with your topic choice and location of information. Be sure to give your parent/guardian advance notice when you need to be driven somewhere. The most successful project is one that is completed by you and not a parent or expert. You will need note cards for taking notes and a pocket folder in which to keep your materials.

One of the goals of this project is to help you develop skills that will assist you with becoming more successful in your academic, and eventually in your business career. Another goal is to help you become more organized. In order to achieve these goals, you will need to do the following: create an outline; compile notes; complete research; write a well-planned paper; document and give credit to all sources; and create a visual display. When doing your research, make sure to use a variety of resources, including, but not limited to, encyclopedias, the Internet, books, and pamphlets. Be sure to ask a parent, guardian, or another adult to proofread your rough draft as well as the final paper.

Be sure to choose a topic that interests you. Make sure you plan your assignments so that all deadlines are met. If you approach this project positively and enthusiastically, you should learn a great deal and have fun in the process.

Decision Making: Topic for Research Project

1. List below are some choices for a Science Fair Project:

 ____

 ____

 ____

2. Ask the following questions for assistance in making a decision, using the choices above. Develop a code to weigh the answers for each question. (For example: Yes, No, or Maybe). Use these answers to decide which topic to choose.

   A. Is this a topic that really interests me?

   B. What are three different sources where I might find information on this topic?

   C. Under which of the Science Fair Categories does this topic belong?

   D. What question can I make from this topic?

   E. Will I be able to test this topic using the scientific method?

3. My Science Fair Project Topic is ______________________________.

4. The reasons I have chosen this topic are as follows (refer to the questions in #2):

   A. ______________________________

   B. ______________________________

   C. ______________________________

   D. ______________________________

Student Signature ______________________________ Date ____________

Parent Signature ______________________________ Date ____________

Research Proposal Sheet

Student's Name: ______________________________ Teacher: ______________________________

SECTION I:

Question: ____

____

Science Category: ____

Hypothesis: ____

____

Teacher Suggestions: ____

____

SECTION II:

Rewritten question: ____

____

Science Category: ____

Hypothesis: ____

____

SECTION III:

List below three different resources you plan to use for your research.

1. ____
2. ____
3. ____

Teacher Suggestions: ____

____

____

Parent Signature ____ Date ______________

Suggested Roles of Responsibility

The successful completion of the Science Fair Project requires much support and assistance. It is strongly advised that all faculty and staff members provide as much support as possible to teachers and students. Listed below are some recommendations for involvement of staff members.

Principal and Administrators:

- Select the date for the local science fair.
- Appoint a committee to plan and coordinate the local science fair.
- Provide certificates for all participants in the science fair.

Faculty and Staff:

- Help students select science fair topics.
- Provide clear communication (in writing) to students and parents.
- Assist in cutting out letters.
- Help students obtain research materials.
- Check the first draft of the research paper and make suggestions for revisions.
- Proofread the final research paper.
- Help with the backboard design.
- Provide encouragement and praise.

Media Specialist:

- Assist students in identifying appropriate resources.
- Serve as a resource teacher for the research paper.
- Work with teachers to schedule time in the media center.

Computer Specialist:

- Assist students in the proper use of computer equipment.
- Help students with appropriate word processing software.
- Supervise student use of the Internet while in the Computer Lab.

Custodians:

- Help with the setup of areas that will be used for project viewing by parents, faculty, staff, and students.

Periodic Table for Reference

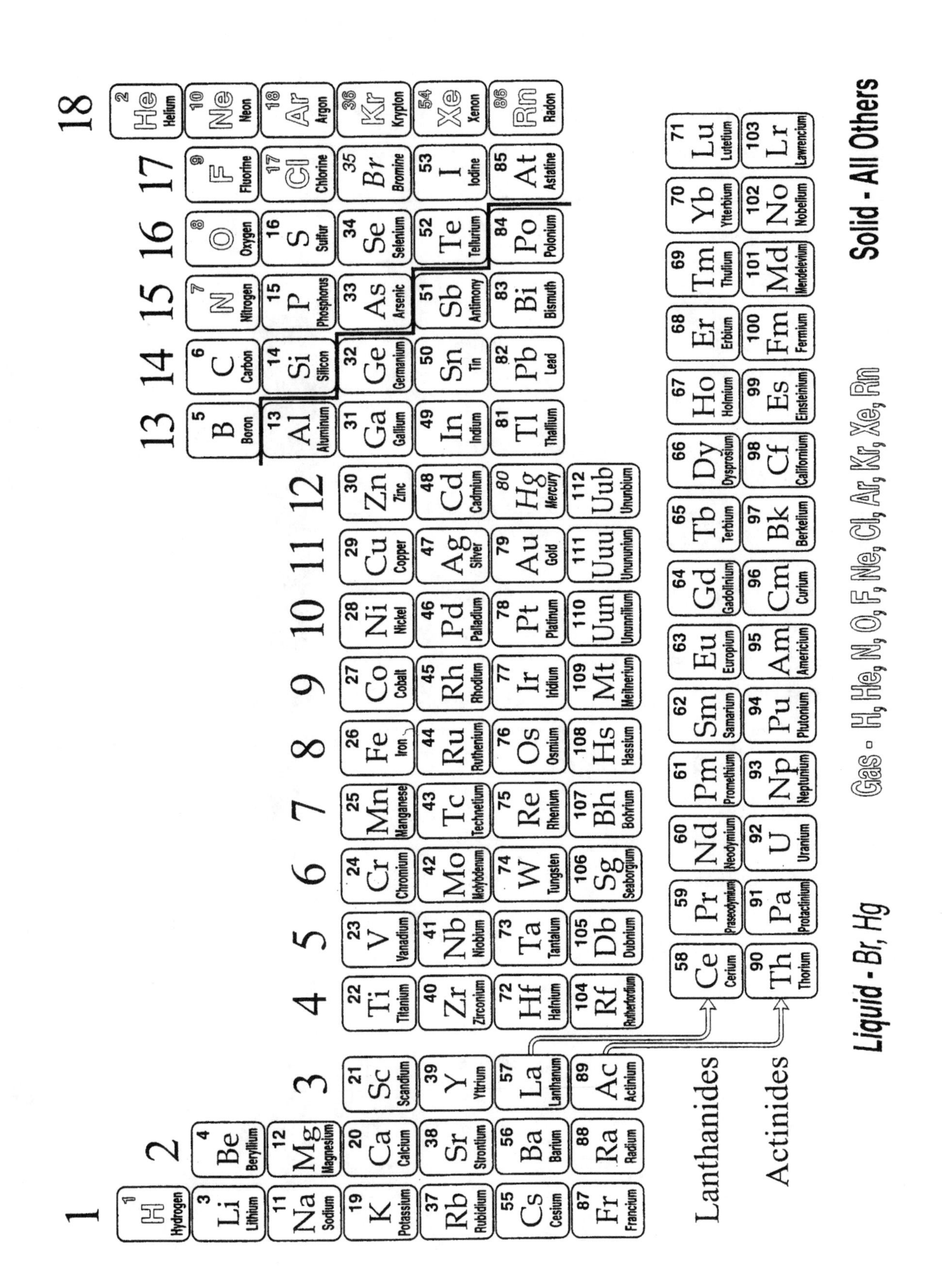

Metric System for Reference: Conversion Chart

Metric to English
Approximate Conversions from Metric Measures

Symbol	*When You Know*	*Multiply By*	*To Find*	*Symbol*
		Length		
mm	millimeters	0.04	inches	in.
cm	centimeters	0.4	inches	in.
m	meters	3.3	feet	ft.
m	meters	1.1	yards	yd.
km	kilometers	0.6	miles	mi.
		Area		
cm^2	square centimeters	0.16	square inches	$in.^2$
m^2	square meters	1.2	square yards	$yd.^2$
km^2	square kilometers	0.4	square miles	$mi.^2$
ha	hectares (10,000 m^2)	2.5	acres	
		Mass/Weight		
g	grams	0.03	ounces	oz.
kg	kilograms	2.2	pounds	lb.
t	tonnes (1,000 kg)	1.1	short tons	
		Volume		
ml	milliliters	0.03	fluid ounces	fl. oz.
l	liters	2.1	pints	pt.
l	liters	1.06	pints	qt.
l	liters	0.26	gallons	gal.
m^3	cubic meters	35	cubic feet	$ft.^3$
m^3	cubic meters	1.3	cubic yards	$yd.^3$
		Temperature (Exact)		
°C	Celsius	$^9/_5$ (then add 32)	Fahrenheit	°F

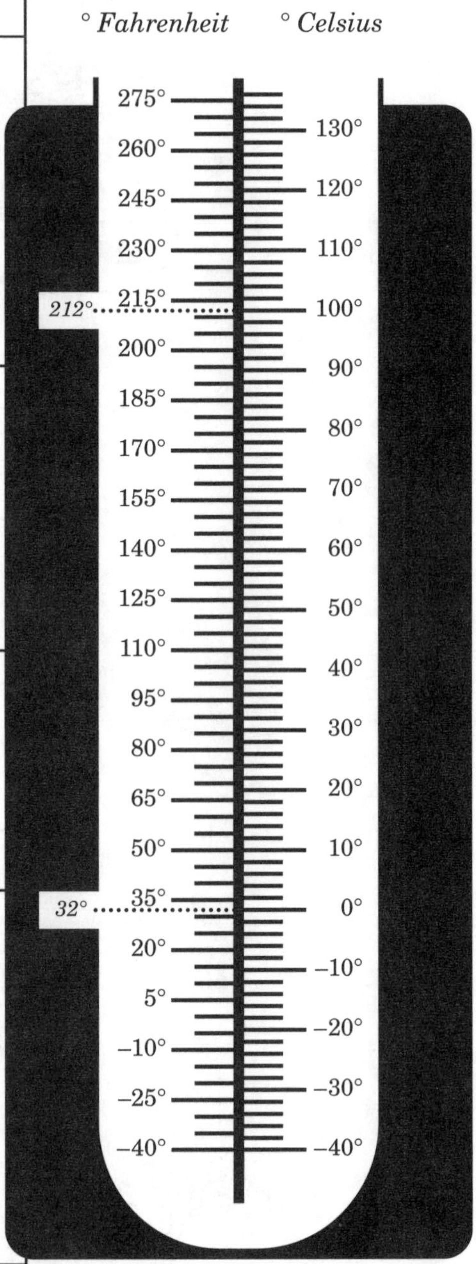

° Fahrenheit ° Celsius

275° 260° 245° 230° 215° 212° 200° 185° 170° 155° 140° 125° 110° 95° 80° 65° 50° 35° 32° 20° 5° –10° –25° –40°

130° 120° 110° 100° 90° 80° 70° 60° 50° 40° 30° 20° 10° 0° –10° –20° –30° –40°

Graphing

During experimentation, utilize an effective method to illustrate results by creating a chart or table of information. This method is a quick and easy way to record results. When all testing is complete, the information can be used to create a line graph or a bar graph. The following is an example of how this may be achieved:

Under What Color Light Do Plants Grow Best?

(Note: data shown is for variable of blue light only.)

Week	Height (in)	Growth (in)
Plants Purchased	5 in.	———
1st Week	6 in.	1 in.
2nd Week	$9\frac{1}{2}$ in.	$3\frac{1}{2}$ in.
3rd Week	13 in.	$3\frac{1}{2}$ in.
4th Week	$15\frac{1}{2}$ in.	2 in.
TOTAL GROWTH	———	10 in.

Notice below how the same information is shown as a bar graph.

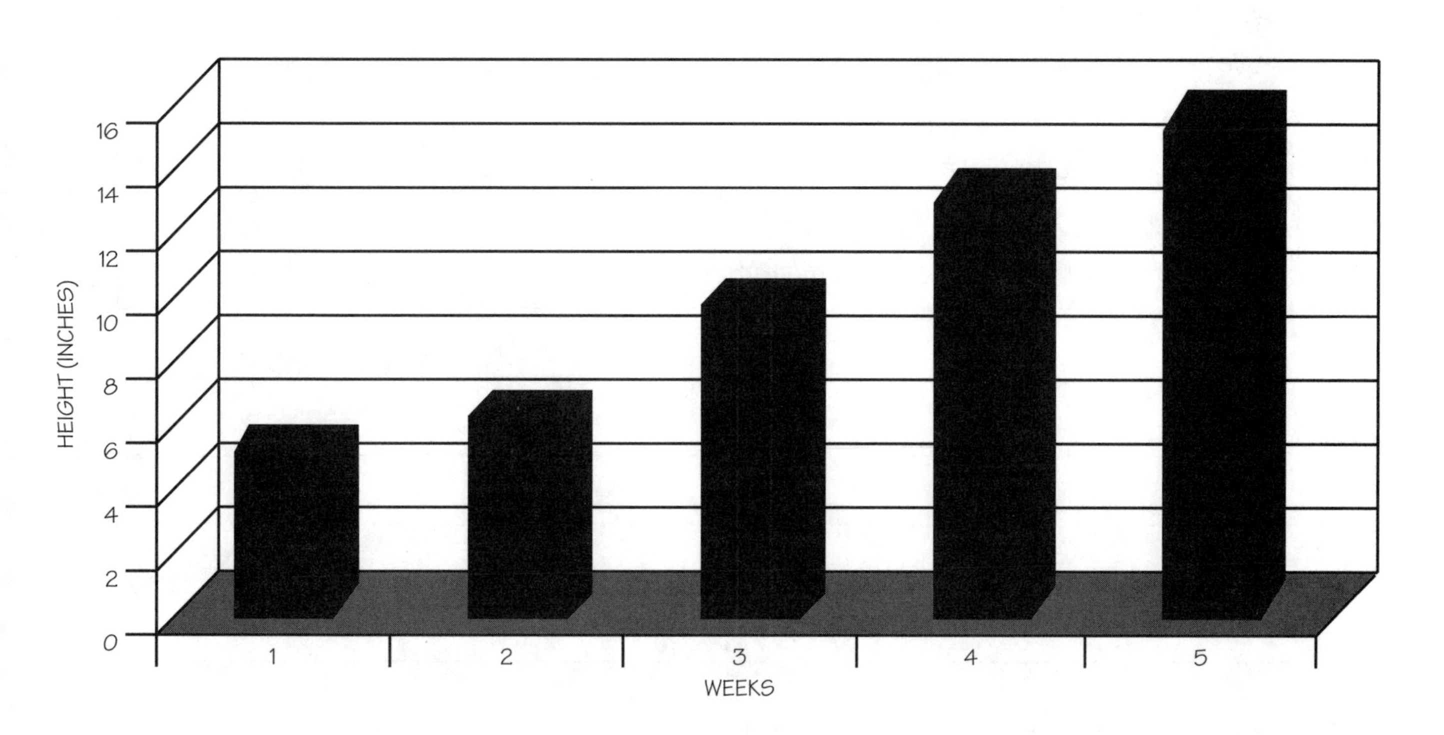

Science Fair Judge's Score Sheet

Judge's No. ______

School ______________________ Date ______________

Student's Name ______________________

Title of Science Project ______________________

Category ______________________ Class ______________

	High Quality	Acceptable	Needs Work
1. Originality of the topic.	10 9 8	7 6 5 4	3 2 1
2. Demonstrates the use of the scientific method.	10 9 8	7 6 5 4	3 2 1
3. Presents scientific data in a well-organized way.	10 9 8	7 6 5 4	3 2 1
4. Shows written evidence of research, experimentation, and analysis.	10 9 8	7 6 5 4	3 2 1
5. Data supports the conclusion.	10 9 8	7 6 5 4	3 2 1
6. Visual display includes all required elements.	10 9 8	7 6 5 4	3 2 1
7. The display is visually appealing.	10 9 8	7 6 5 4	3 2 1
8. The log book entries are dated, written in ink, and organized.	10 9 8	7 6 5 4	3 2 1
9. All components of the project are included and complete.	10 9 8	7 6 5 4	3 2 1
10. All parts of the science project have correct spelling, punctuation, and grammar.	10 9 8	7 6 5 4	3 2 1

Total Points = ______

Positive Comments: ______________________

____

Suggestions: ______________________

____

____

Checklist for the Completed Project

	Yes	No
1. Is the research question appropriate for the topic?		
2. Did student follow the scientific method?		
3. Is the abstract written clearly and correctly?		
4. Does the written report include:		
a. Title Page		
b. Table of Contents		
c. Outline		
d. Introductory Paragraph		
e. Materials & Procedures		
f. Results		
g. Discussion		
h. Conclusion		
i. Credits		
j. Bibliography		
k. Appendix (if needed)		
5. Does the log book contain the following:		
a. Dated Entries		
b. Section Dividers		
c. Notes on Readings & Bibliographic Information		
d. Raw Data		
6. Does the backboard include:		
a. A Clearly Written Title		
b. The Purpose of my Experimentation		
c. My Hypothesis		
d. The Researched Problem		
e. Observations		
f. Results		
g. Materials & Procedures		
h. Conclusion		
7. Is the name and other required information included on both the research paper and the display?		
8. Has someone proofread the research paper and checked the backboard for spelling and other grammatical errors?		
9. Is the exhibit attractive, educational, and appealing?		

Science Fair Project: Websites

Agricultural Ideas for Science Fair Projects

http://www.ars.usda.gov/is/kids/fair/ideasframe.htm

Agriculture does not have its own category in science fairs, but it is a part of many of the "official" categories. Here, we have put together a few basic ideas of agricultural science projects you can do. Use these ideas as "jumping-off" points for coming up with your own project.

Carolina Biological Supply Company

http://www.carolina.com

Use this source to locate science equipment and supplies.

CHEMetrics, Inc.

http://www.chemetrics.com

This source is a supplier of chemical kits.

Cyber Fair: Idea Generation

http://www.isd77.k12.mn.us/resources/cf/ideas.html

This site offers tips and sample topics as a starting point. This allows the student to explore and find interesting ideas.

How to Get Started?

http://www.twingroves.district96.k12.il.us/ScienceInternet/GetStarted.html

This source guides students through the steps of choosing a topic, including how to narrow down a topic. Also, the site includes ways to find project ideas along with some simple exercises in how to frame an idea into a research question.

LaMotte Chemical Products Company

http://www.lamotte.com

Necessary project materials can be ordered from this chemical company.

Science Fair Project: Websites

Nasco

http://www.nascofa.com

Nasco is an excellent resource for hundreds of science products.

Science Fair Central: Project Ideas

http://school.discovery.com/sciencefaircentral/scifairstudio/ideas.html

This site breaks down ideas into various topic areas.

Science Fairs

http://www.stemnet.nf.ca/sciencefairs/

Science Fairs offers numerous scientific categories from which to choose, and provides a number of project ideas in each category.

U.S. Department of Labor

http://www.osha.gov

Use this resource to locate guidelines and regulations regarding animal research projects and laboratory safety.

U.S. Fish & Wildlife Service

http://endangered.fws.gov/esa.html

This resource may be used to research federal laws concerning endangered species.

United States Geological Survey

http://www.usgs.gov/

This home page includes an index of online resources concerning earth science.

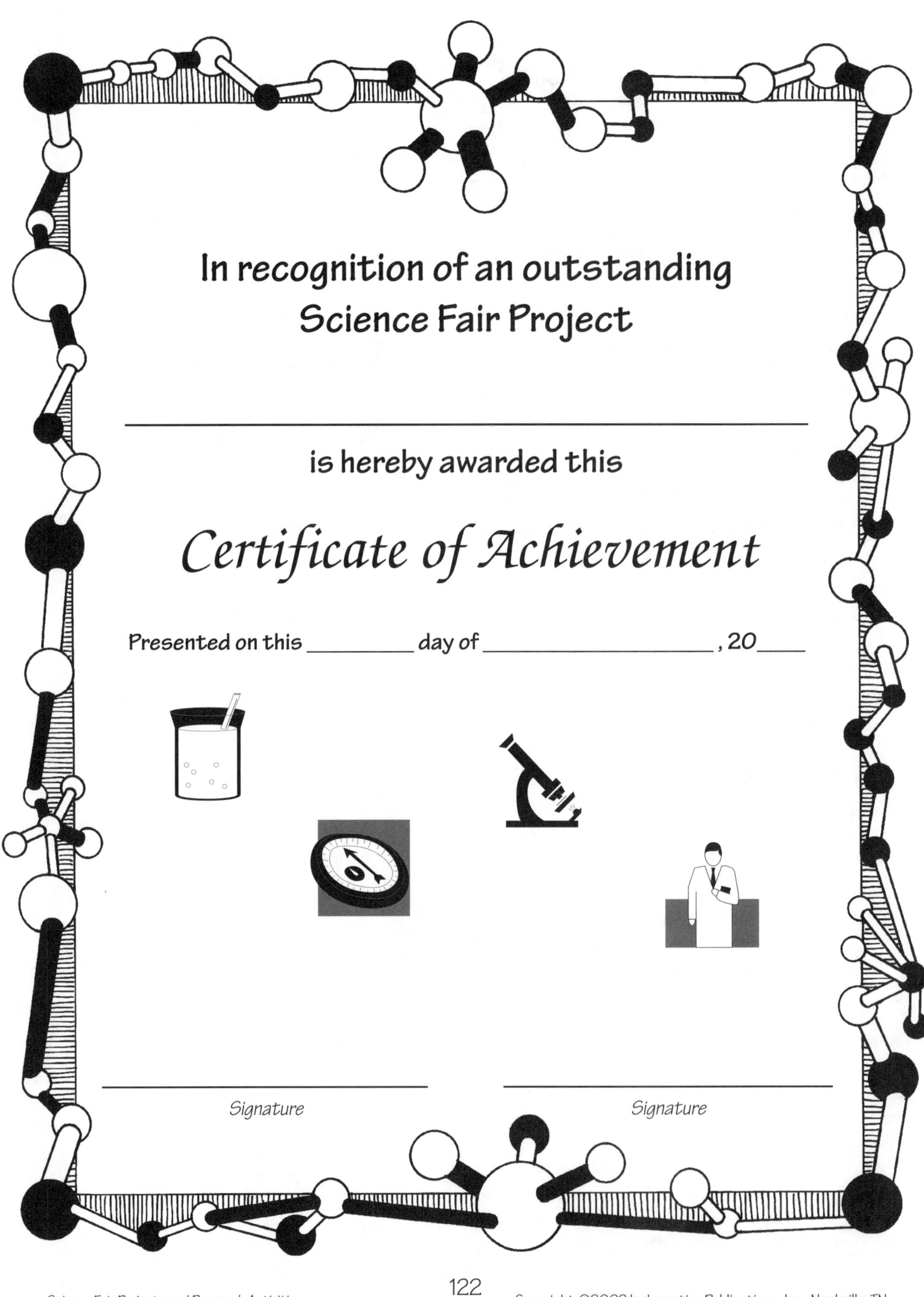
In recognition of an outstanding
Science Fair Project
is hereby awarded this
Certificate of Achievement
Presented on this ________ day of ____________________, 20____
Signature
Signature

Answer Key

Recognizing Poor Science Topics

The topics below are poor choices for a science fair project. On the line beneath each topic, write the reason why it should not be chosen.

1. What elements comprise water?
   topic is limited
2. What would be the best way to improve things?
   too broad and too confusing
3. What is an erupting volcano?
   topic is limited
4. Ants in our environment.
   too confusing

Creating a Good Topic

Directions: In order to create a good topic, complete each question by filling in the blanks.
Examples: How do various types of water affect the growth of plants?
What effect does salt have on the boiling point of various liquids?
Which type of seed do birds prefer?

5. How do /does *moisture* affect *growth of molds* ?
6. What effect do /does *fertilizers* have on *plant growth* ?
7. Which type of *treats* do *cats* prefer?
8. What *types of shoes* are preferred by *teenagers* ?
9. Which *battery* lasts longest?
10. Which *detergent* is more effective for *removing stains* ?

PAGE 21

Practice Note Taking

Use your judgment in choosing the most important and least important statements. Read the article carefully, then answer the questions that follow.

Food and Game Fish

Fish is one of the most nourishing foods. The amount of protein found in fish is about the same as that found in meat. Every year, several million tons of tuna, cod, herring, and other ocean food fish are caught by commercial fishermen. There are also many inland waters where commercial fishing takes place. Salmon, trout, and perch are some types of freshwater food fish.

The business of fish farming is called aquaculture. Fish farms raise fish for food. In the United States salmon, catfish, and trout are raised on fish farms. In other countries in the world, fish and carp are raised in fish farms. Ponds are used by fish farmers for raising the fish. They use special feeding methods to grow fish larger and faster than they would grow in the wild.

Many people enjoy fishing for fun. They like to go after game fish. They include swordfish and marlin in the ocean and trout and bass in fresh water. Game fish are exciting to catch because of their size and fighting spirit.

1. What are two results of using special feeding methods in fish farming?
   The fish grow larger and they grow faster.
2. What is so nourishing about fish?
   It has the same amount of protein as meat.
3. Name three types of fish raised on fish farms in the United States.
   salmon, catfish, and trout
4. What is so exciting about catching game fish?
   The excitement comes because game fish are so large and have such a fighting spirit.

PAGE 43

Practice Note Taking

When taking notes, begin by skimming the material in order to get a general idea of the content. When reading the material for the second time, read more carefully in order to find the main points and details. Instead of writing complete sentences, make brief notes.

On the right side of this page, take notes on the article below. Remember to use brief notes instead of complete sentences. Check the article for main ideas, cue words, and punctuation. Remember to use quotation marks for direct quotes.

The Mongolian Gerbil	Notes
There are approximately one hundred species of gerbils. They are found in the dry areas of Asia and Africa. The most well-known type is the Mongolian gerbil.	*100 species of gerbils* *found in dry areas: Asia, Africa* *Mongolian: most well-known*
It makes a good pet for the following reasons: its calm nature, its interesting behavior, and its curiosity.	*Good pet - calm nature, interesting behavior, curiosity*
The Mongolian gerbil is approximately 8 inches long and weighs about 3 ounces. On the tip of its tail is a tuft of black hair. The Mongolian gerbil ranges in color from yellow to brown or gray. Its feet have strong, black or dark brown claws. The Mongolian who normally walks on four legs sometimes hops like a kangaroo, using only its hind legs.	*Description - length 8 in; weight 3 oz; tip of tail black; color gray, yellow, or brown; claws black or dark brown; walks or hops on hind legs*
In the wild, these gerbils are found in parts of Russia and China as well as throughout parts of Mongolia. They live in groups which form colonies and they burrow in the ground for shelter. These gerbils are active during daylight hours as well as evening hours. Their main sources of food include seeds, roots, leaves, bulbs, and stems.	*Location - Russia, China, Mongolia* *- Form colonies* *- Burrow in ground for shelter* *- Active during day and night* *- Food sources: seeds, roots, leaves, bulbs & stems*
Mongolian gerbils can reproduce when they are only ten to twelve weeks old. The female gerbil carries the unborn babies for twenty-four to twenty-six days. The female gerbil may produce as many as twelve babies at a time but normally produces an average of four.	*- Reproduction at 10–12 weeks; carry babies 24–26 days; may have 4–12 babies*

PAGE 44

Outlining Practice

After reading the story on spiders, complete the following outline.

Spiders and Their Webs

I. Spiders' Silk
   A. *Silk Making*
      1. *Spinnerets*
      2. *Sticky Thread*
   B. *Silk Uses*
      1. *Escape*
      2. *Nest*
      3. *Mummies*
      4. *Egg Sac*

II. Web Types
   A. *Tangled Web*
   B. *Sheet Web*
   C. *Round Web*

PAGE 48

Answer Key

Outlining Practice

To further test outline knowledge, parts of two outlines are given below. The outlines are in scrambled order. For the first outline (on the left), the form is supplied. For the second outline, create the form from scratch.

Measuring of Time	Main Sequence Stars
Formation of Stars	Change and Death of Stars
Stars in the Universe	Distance of Stars
Mystery Stars	Binary Stars
Learning from the Stars	Measuring of Direction
Kinds of Stars	
Number of Stars	

Suggestion: Put the Roman numerals first for each of the three main topics. Then leave spaces for the subtopics under each main topic.

Uses of Corn	Milling
Distilling	Sweet Corn
Flour Corn	Livestock Feed
Food for Humans	Flint Corn
Processing of Corn	Feed Manufacturing
Kinds of Corn	Dent Corn

Studying the Stars

I. *Stars in the Universe*
 A. *Number of Stars*
 B. Size of Stars
 C. *Distance of Stars*
II. Use of the Stars
 A. *Measuring of Time*
 B. *Measuring of Direction*
 C. *Learning from the Stars*
III. *Kinds of Stars*
 A. *Mystery Stars*
 B. Variable Stars
 C. *Main-Sequence Stars*
 D. *Binary Stars*
IV. The Birth and Death of Stars
 A. *Formation of Stars*
 B. *Change & Death of Stars*

Growing Corn

I. Kinds of Corn
 A. Flour Corn
 B. Sweet Corn
 C. Flint Corn
 D. Dent Corn
II. Processing of Corn
 A. Distilling
 B. Milling
 C. Feed Manufacturing
III. Uses of Corn
 A. Humans' Food
 B. Livestock Feed

Copyright ©2002 by Incentive Publications, In... Science Fair Projects and Research Activities

PAGE 49

---

e best way to explain what will be learned from the scientific investigation is to write ...stion. The next step is to guess what will happen in the experiment. Scientists call ...guess a *hypothesis*. A clearly written hypothesis answers the question and is brief ...o the point. The following is an example:

Topic: Factors That Affect Tooth Decay
...uestion: Which liquid causes teeth to decay faster?
...othesis: Orange juice will cause a tooth to decay faster than other liquids.

...e a hypothesis for each of the following questions.

...What are the effects of bleach and dye on hair?
...ypothesis: *Bleach and dye will cause hair to become brittle.*

...Which type of food molds the fastest?
...ypothesis: *Fruit molds the fastest.*

...What are the effects of cola on teeth?
...ypothesis: *Cola will cause holes to form in teeth.*

...Does the use of computers improve student performance?
...ypothesis: *Computers will improve student performance.*

...Does soil type change how well plants grow?
...ypothesis: *Plants will grow better in humus.*

...What factors affect the bounce of a dropped ball?
...ypothesis: *The smoother the surface, the higher a ball bounces.*

...Which mouthwash kills the most microbes?
...ypothesis: *"Fresh Breath" will kill the most microbes.*

...Which types of treats do dogs prefer?
...ypothesis: *Dogs prefer treats with meat flavor.*

...t ©2002 by Incentive Publications, Inc., Nashville, TN. 53 Science Fair Projects and Research Activities

PAGE 53

Experimental Studies

In experimental studies, examine all of the factors that might change an experiment. Alter certain conditions and then observe how they affect the experiment. The conditions that are altered are called variables. There are two types of variables, independent and dependent. An independent variable is one that is purposely changed before the experiment. A dependent variable is one that must be measured and recorded during the experiment.

In a **controlled** experiment, two groups may be needed: the experimental group in which only one variable is changed at a time; and the control group in which there are no variables. On the other hand, the science project may not require a control group.

Two hypotheses are listed below. For each hypothesis, name the variable that would be changed to help solve the hypothesis. Then list the controlled variables that would stay the same for every test. The first hypothesis has been completed as an example to follow.

Hypothesis I: *"Wrap-It" Plastic Wrap will be the strongest.*
Independent Variable: Different brands of plastic wrap
Dependent Variable: The strength of the different plastic wraps
Controls: Same size test sheet, same weight, same amount of time

Hypothesis II: *"Orange Juice will cause a tooth to decay faster than other liquids."*
Independent Variable: *various liquids used for example: cola, orange juice, milk, water*
Dependent Variable: *tooth decay*
Controls: *equal amounts of liquid in container, same size containers, kept in same refrigerator, liquid changed weekly, same amount replaced.*

Science Fair Projects and Research Activities ...02 by Incentive Publications, Inc., Nashville, TN.

PAGE 54

Experimental Design Practice

Use the experiments described on pages 51–52 or one that the teacher assigns to complete the following form:

☑ Problem
Does practice improve distance jumped?

☑ Hypothesis
Practice will improve distance jumped.

☑ Materials
pencil, ruler, calendar, masking tape, data table

☑ Independent Variable(s)
the number of times drop jumping is done for practice

☑ Dependent Variable
the height of the vertical jump

☑ Control
same time of day, same place, same method of measuring height

Copyright ©2002 by Incentive Publications, In... Science Fair Projects and Research Activities

PAGE 55

Answer Key

Introductory Paragraph Practice

While writing the introductory paragraph, please keep in mind that the introduction should include background information and the reasons for the choice of study. Conclude by stating the hypothesis.

Directions: Edit the first draft paragraph. While rewriting the paragraph, feel free to change any of the words, place the sentences in a more logical order, and remove any sentences that do not agree with the main topic. Also correct any errors in spelling, capitalization, and punctuation.

My hypothisis for the experiments was: if the water is more pure, then the plant will sprout faster. I picked this topic simply out of curioseity. It was because since some of my neighbors water their plants with water, I was wondering if it makes a diference about which type of water you use. My topic is about whether or not it depends if the type of water makes seeds sprout faster. The topic also relates to many agricultural spots and how plants thrive. I wanted to know what is the difference between the types of water was made. It was interesting enough. I used distilled water, spring water, mineral water, tap water, and salt water.

Does the type of water used affect the sprouting of seeds? The reason I chose this topic was simply out of curiosity. After observing various neighbors caring for their plants, I wondered if the type of water used would affect the speed of sprouting seeds. I was also curious about the types of water available and how each type of water is made. When I conducted my experiments, I used distilled water, spring water, mineral water, tap water, and salt water. Therefore, my hypothesis, based on the research that I did, was the purer the water, the quicker the seed will sprout.

PAGE 69

Conclusion Practice

Remember that the concluding paragraph should briefly summarize results. It should include discussion of whether or not the data supported the hypothesis. Finally, include what the next steps in experimentation may be.

Directions: Read the following conclusion. Feel free to change any of the words, place the sentences in a more logical order, and remove any sentences that do not agree with the main topic. Also, correct any errors in spelling, capitalization, and punctuation.

The substence that reached the boiling point the fastest was the BBQ sauce. Does the size of a pot have an effect on the speed at which a substance comes to its boiling point.

I beleive the BBQ sauce heated quicker because it are thicker and its molecules are closer together. I really like BBQ sauce because of its zingy taste. Therefore, my hypothisis were incorrect. I assume that this is the case be cause mollecules of water are farther apart. This experiment lead me to another question:

The substance that reached the boiling point the fastest was the BBQ sauce. Therefore, my hypothesis was incorrect.

I believe that the BBQ sauce heated more quickly because it is thicker, and its molecules are closer together. I assume that the water did not come to a boil as quickly because its molecules are farther apart.

This experiment led me to another question: Does the size of the pot have any effect on the speed at which a substance reaches its boiling point?

PAGE 70

Abstract Practice

When writing your abstract, remember that an abstract is a concise summary of the entire research project. It should include the following: purpose, hypothesis, procedure, data, conclusions, and possible applications.

Directions: Edit the following abstract. While rewriting the abstract, feel free to change any of the words, place the sentences in a more logical order, and remove any sentences that do not agree with the main topic. Also, correct any errors in spelling, capitalization, and punctuation.

The porpuse of this experiment was to find out which substance from the ones in my experiment reached the boiling point the fastest. Procedures. 1) place of the substances on each of the boiling pots. 2) turn the stove on to mediuim. 3. place four of the boiling pots to heat up. 5) write on your log book the time at which each substance was placed to a boil. 5) write down the time at which each substance begins to bubble or reach boiling point. 6) repeat steps a, b, c, and e. Data: the substance that reached boiling point the qucikest was the BBQ sauce with four minutes, then water with five minutes and 28 secs. then water with salt with five minutes and 58 secs. then water water with oil with 6 minutes and 20 seconds and finally milk with nine minutes. Conclusion: in conclusion the substance that reaches boiling point the quickest was water. Reference: Books of Science

The purpose of this experiment was to determine which substance reaches the boiling point the fastest. The following procedures were used in the experimentation. Measure the first substance and place it in a pot. Begin to heat the pot, recording the time. When the substance boils, record the time again. Repeat this procedure for each substance.

The BBQ sauce boiled after 4 minutes. The water boiled after 5 minutes and 58 seconds. After 6 minutes and 28 seconds the water with oil boiled. Finally, the milk boiled after 9 minutes. The BBQ sauce boiled fastest because it is thicker and its molecules are closer to each other.

PAGE 71

Writing Bibliographical Entries

When writing a research paper, it is necessary to include a bibliography at the end. The bibliography is a list of all the sources used when gathering information for the paper. Bibliographies follow a special format and list important information about the sources. Write bibliographical entries for the sources listed below. As a guide, refer to pages 76–77.

1. A book called Poison Ivy was written by Ann Tehis Tamean and published by Don T. Scratch Publishing Company, of Rashville, in 1999.

   Tamean, Ann Tehis. Poison Ivy. Nashville: Don T. Scratch Publishing, 1999.

2. "Static Electricity" written by Rub de Fabric was found online and published by Spark Publishers in Electron City, on May 3, 2000.

   Fabric, Rub de. "Static Electricity." Online. Electron City: Spark Publishers, May 3, 2000.

3. A pamphlet entitled Water Conservation by Dri P. Faucets was produced by The American Plumbing Corporation in Springfield in 2001.

   Faucets, Dri P. Water Conservation. Springfield: The American Plumbing Corporation, 2001.

4. Appearing in Vol. 26 of Bright Light Encyclopedia in 1997 was an article on "Solar Power" written by Sunny Day and found on pages 127–129.

   Day, Sunny. "Solar Power." Bright Light Encyclopedia. Volume 26, 1997: 127–129

PAGE 78

Answer Key

5. Published by Green Thumb Publishing Company of Elm City, Rosie Bush wrote an article entitled "Growing Green" for Plant Life Magazine in August of 1999.

Bush, Rosie. "Growing Green." Plant Life Magazine. August, 1999.

6. Mitochondrian Times contained an article in Section C, page 2 on "Cell Structure" written by Cyto Plasm and produced by Nucleus Publisher on February 12, 1997.

Plasm, Cyto. "Cell Structure." Mitochondrian Times. February 12, 1997: Sec C, p. 2.

7. A book on Bionomial Classification was jointly written by Ollie Gee and Carol S. Linnaeus and published by Genus & Species, New York in 1998.

Gee, Ollie and Carol S. Linnaeus. Binomial Classification. New York: Genus & Species, 1998.

8. A. M. Plified was interviewed by S. Ound Waves at 11:00 AM on August 10, 2001 in Speakerville, New Hampshire.

Plified, A. M. Speakerville, New Hampshire. Aug 10, 2001.

9. I received an e-mail through Catchmet, entitled "Food Chain" on June 25, 2000. Bengal Ty Ger wrote it on May 24, 2000. It was then received from Predatorgroup.comp.hungry.eat.prey.

Ger, Bengal Ty. "Food Chain." [Online] Available e-mail: Predatorgroup.comp.hungry.eat.prey. May 24, 2000.

PAGE 79

Bibliography Practice

Blake really needs help writing a bibliographic list. He used the sources listed in the paragraph below while writing his science research paper: "How Can Hydrogen Be Used to Produce Large Amounts of Energy." For the bibliography, use the lines below.

In the book Test Tubes and Beakers by E. H. Coulson, A. E. Trinder, and Aaron E. Klein, Blake found information. The book was published by Doubleday in New York in 1971. He also found an article entitled "Hydrolysis" in Encarta Encyclopedia produced by Microsoft Corporation in 1993. The third source was the book Designated Supervisor written by Pavel Chterev in 2001 and published by Graham Publishing of Atlanta. He found an article entitled The Polarity of Water on the internet at http://biology.arizona.edu/biochemistry/tutorials/page3/html. Finally, Blake located an article entitled "Hydrogen" in the Encyclopedia Britannica, Vol. 7, pages 206–208. It was published in 1999.

Bibliography

Chterev, Pavel. Designated Supervisor. Atlanta: Graham Publishing, 2001.

Coulson, E. H., A. E. Trinder, and Aaron E. Klein. Test Tubes and Beakers. New York: Doubleday, 1971.

"Hydrogen." Encyclopedia Britannica. Vol. 7. pages 206–208.

"Hydrolysis." Encarta Encyclopedia. Microsoft Corporation, 1993.

"The Polarity of Water." Internet. http://biology.arizona.edu/biochemistry/tutorials/page3/html

PAGE 80

Science Fair Project Title Cards

Note to the Teacher: *Reproduce these title cards on card stock and give to each student doing a science project.*

PURPOSE

HYPOTHESIS

PROBLEM

OBSERVATIONS

RESULTS

MATERIALS

PROCEDURES

CONCLUSION

GRAPH CHART